Social Media:
Your Child's Digital Tattoo

Stephen J Smith

ISBN:
ISBN-9781549598647

DEDICATION

For my wonderful wife and best-friend Mary Beth, and our children, Beth and Jenni; grandkids Stephen, Maria, Liam, Emily, Kenzie and son-in-law Jason.
Without your love, kindness, and support, this book would not have been possible.
Love,
Steve, Dad, Poppy

TABLE OF CONTENTS

Foreword..1

Chapter 1 – A Distracted Society 14

Chapter 2 – The Consequences Of Sending Inappropriate Content 23

Chapter 3 – How And Why Our Private Information Is Invaded 45

Chapter 4 - Self Esteem, Stalking, Cat Fishing & Divorce.................88

Chapter 5 – Pornography..112

Chapter 6 – Mental Health 120

Chapter 7 – Managing Your Child's Online Activity 142

Chapter 8: Conclusion 155

Research References 157

About The Author..171

Acknowledgments

I want to acknowledge the many students, teachers, counselors, psychologists, psychiatrists, nurses, pediatricians, principals and school resource officers that have worked with me over the past five years in helping families understand how social media can impact the lives of our youth. Without their help, this book would not be possible.

However, I also want to thank the many prosecutors that have worked with me in a seven county area in Ohio, Indiana and Kentucky. Many times these fine people worked extra hours presenting to schools – only to then drive back to their offices to complete their already busy work days.

In particular, I want to thank Steve Franzen, Kentucky's Campbell County Attorney and, Dotty Smith, Chief Assistant Prosecutor, Municipal/Juvenile Divisions of the

Clermont County Prosecutor's Office. Steve and Dotty took the time to review their past cases so that I could include real-life legal experiences with teens that had misused technology. Their help, professionalism and kindness are greatly appreciated.

Foreword

The Digital Landscape

I have always had a fascination with stories related to unintended consequences. Hollywood is ripe with story lines of young men falling in love with beautiful women, only to discover the relationship deteriorating to a tempest of tipping dominos and unlikely sub plots.

The same is often true with technology. We need to look no further than our country's battle with growth following the Revolutionary War. The subsequent economic crisis challenged the future stability of a young country. The war was won, but another battle ensued.

For example, in 1863 there was Joseph Wilbrand who, while attempting to develop a yellow dye, discovered trinitrotoluene. However, it was soon determined that trinitrotoluene had rather enormous explosive and destructive power. By 1902, under the name in which we are all familiar, i.e., TNT – the chemical became used extensively during the two World Wars to kill and conqueror.

Then, of course, there was Thomas Midgley, who like me is a former NCR employee, who later became an executive at DELCO and discovered Chlorofluorocarbon Freon as a safe refrigerant to replace the commonly used but highly toxic refrigerant ammonia. We know this discovery today as CFCs — which have caused extensive damage to the Ozone Layer.

Midgley later went on to discover that adding tetraethyl lead to gasoline to be a remedy for engine knocking. As we all know today that discovery led to global health and environmental issues that include deaths from lead poisoning and severe damage to our environment. Mr. Midgley's own death was due in large part to his exposure to such chemicals.

So, it is not surprising that today is no different. One discovery begets yet another use or creates a complication not formerly considered.

I had to laugh while driving into my office awhile back when hearing the story of an Indiana Farmer losing a lawsuit to Monsanto. The farmer had apparently purchased soybean seeds that were marketed for feeding livestock. However, knowing that the seed was harvested from genetically enhanced soybean plants that were impervious to certain weed killers, he decided to plant the seeds rather than feed them to livestock. He later saved the resulting soybean plants to be sold – while also harvesting some of the seeds for replanting and then growing in subsequent years.

His thinking: Why pay for a product each year if it can actually reproduce itself?

According to the <u>Wall Street Journal</u>, *"The court unanimously found that farmer Vernon Bowman violated Monsanto's patent on herbicide-resistant soybean seeds by using them to grow successive generations of similarly endowed crops, rather than consuming or selling the seeds."*

To put it simply, if you replace the word soybean with music, Mr. Bowman "was stealing copyrighted material." By purchasing one version of the seed and replicating it – he had somewhat created the "the agrarian version of Napster." Well... Maybe that's a stretch.

We are truly living in a new world. While most of us know that it is illegal to download music from iTunes and then make multiple copies for your friends — who would have thought that soybean seeds were the equivalent of software licenses?

To that end, who would have thought that the large, awkward cell phones that we see on syndicated shows like Seinfeld would have evolved into the small, powerful devices we use today to play games, communicate with friends and family and post videos on places like Facebook, Instagram and Snap Chat?

This evolution of technology also requires an evolution in parenting skills. Parenting today is a much different animal than in years past. For example, I can recall purchasing our oldest daughter a cell phone when she turned 16 and began driving. Our rationale related to safety. If there were an accident or flat tire, she'd simply give us a call.

Four years later when our youngest daughter turned 16, text messaging had begun to grow in popularity. By 2002 text messaging became ubiquitous due in part to it being agnostic concerning wireless carriers. It allowed a user to multitask without regard to time constraints – and it was very portable. You could send a text during a movie; while in a meeting; from the backseat of your parent's car –or, from just about anywhere at any time.

Soon, text messages became the primary means by which young people communicated, eclipsing voice calls by a wide margin. However, just like Joseph Wilbrand's synthetic yellow dye -- which ultimately became better known for its explosive characteristics — today's wireless technology has had its share of unintended consequences.

Seven years ago, I would not have thought that teens would send naked pictures of themselves using text messages. Yet today, about 25% - 30% of teens have used the technology for this purpose now known as sexting.

Although bullying has existed since the days of the Neanderthals – did we understand that cell phones would be used in some cases to humiliate, bully and intimidate other young people?

Did we understand that social media sites and apps would open the world up to our children – while opening our kids up to the world?

Did we think about these issues before handing the

4

phone or tablet over to our children without any education or boundaries?

As of this writing in July 2017, I have spoken to nearly 300,000 students and adults on the issues related to technology. In the five years that we have been making these presentations much has changed.

According to our 2016 survey of teens and their use of smartphones, the average teen will admit to spending over 3 hours per day on smartphones and tablets. Some of them much, much more. The majority of this time is on a mobile device – often outside the home.

What does this mean to parents? Simply put, the way our youth culture communicates is significantly different than even 5-10 years ago. While much of this change is for good, it is incumbent upon us as parents and grandparents to understand and monitor the technology that our children and grandchildren are using.

I have often used the analogy of New York City when discussing technology. I first traveled to New York in 1982. It was the biggest and most fascinating city to which I had traveled. It had the best art, music venues, food and diversity of culture I had experienced. But I would never allow my child to visit New York without being accompanied by my wife and me.

As I discovered on my first visit — it's easy to get lost in New York. It is easy to turn down the wrong street at the wrong time. Grabbing a cab back to LaGuardia at 4:00 pm is almost impossible. There were merchants selling so called "authentic" Gucci and Rolex products at steep discounts.

And there were very friendly young ladies offering to escort me around the city for "a good time." I felt much like Gomer Pyle transported from Mayberry to Times Square. I was not prepared. I didn't know the rules of engagement.

The internet, which was at one time limited to clunky desktops in your family-room is now available 7 x 24 on your child's phone. Much like New York, the Internet is a fascinating place to visit. But you need to be prepared and understand how to get around. You need to know the sites and apps that you access – and the people that don't have your best interest at heart.

Additionally, there has been an explosion of growth in smartphone apps. While we often think that the Internet is the biggest of our concerns, the reality is that Apps and Bots might represent the biggest challenge for parents. Smartphone apps such as Instagram and Snap Chat are often unknown to parents. In fact, in recent presentations, I have asked the question, "How many of you have heard of WhatsApp?" The majority of parents had no idea what it was. However, when we asked students, "How many of you are using WhatsApp?" The overwhelming majority of the students raised their hands in affirmation.

Ask parents about Bots, and the room goes silent. We'll discuss those later in this book.

How can you keep up with this constant evolution? Well, this book is a start. We also suggest that you visit our website, www.awiredfamily.org. Much of the content of this book was published on that site. I encourage you

6

to access the site periodically to understand the apps that kids are using; the websites they're accessing; the new technologies they're using and the fads related to these technologies.

So, what is your child's digital tattoo? It is the accumulation of data and metadata about your child's likes, dislikes, comments, pictures, current and historical location and many other items related to what your child does on their digital devices. Most of us would have probably thought twice before providing these devices to our children -- had we only known the endless information that our kids give up to marketing companies based on their use of free apps and bots.

Although many of us have a real tattoo on our skin, most had given the tattoo great thought before going through the pain and cost of going under the needle. We selected the design. Decided where the tattoo would exist on our bodies. We decided who the artist would be and what possible consequences there would be for getting a tattoo.

In today's world, unless you get a face tattoo, few professions would be unavailable to you. Regardless, the tattoo was your decision.

With digital tattoos, your child did not decide to get one. They don't know where it is. They don't know who can see it. They don't know what the consequences will be for having the digital tattoo.

Our point? If your child is using an app, website or digital device, they are creating a digital tattoo. If curated properly, that information can benefit your child. If your

*child does not properly curate their social media activity –
it can create obstacles to their future success. This book
will guide you through that digital landscape and great
evolution in communications so that your child's online
activity doesn't hinder their future endeavors.*

Several years ago, when I came home from work, I sat
on the couch with my wife, Mary Beth, watching the local
news. One of the stories involved a young lady that had
just taken her own life. Although teen suicides at that
time were not unheard of – the underlying reason for this
death was unusual for 2008. The story caught my
attention and my heart.

Months earlier, the young lady in the story had taken a
naked photo and sent it to her boyfriend. Following their
breakup, he sent that picture to girls in the school. Before
long, hundreds of people had this embarrassing photo.

The resulting harassment and bullying she received
turned this once attractive and vivacious young lady into
a shadow of her former self. Her depression grew until
she could finally take it no more. She hung herself in her
bedroom to escape the pain.

Having lost our grandson eight days following his birth,
my wife and I relived the sting of loss through the eyes of
the mother and father who had just lost their only child
to suicide. However, our grandson died of a medical
condition. It was unavoidable. This young lady ended her
own life – a tragedy that as we know, after many years of
researching the impact of technology on children – was
entirely avoidable.

The next day I went to our management and suggested

we develop an education program for students and parents on the issues related to the misuse of technology. Although this is where the story began, it has evolved over the years as technology, and its use has changed. In 2008, when that young lady took her photo, she used a flip phone. Today, the overwhelming majority of students use smartphones.

The first iPhone launched in 2007. The Android didn't even exist until October of 2008.

In 2007 there were 552 apps available in the iTunes Store. By 2008, Apple opened up the store to 3rd parties to develop apps. By 2009, there were over 500 million apps downloaded by users.

According to Statistica, by March of 2017, there were over 2.2 million apps available in the iTunes Store and 2.8 million available in Google Play. The world has changed dramatically in just ten years.

According to e-marketer, as of 2016, 75% of teens have a smartphone. Moreover, from my own experience in middle schools, the majority of 5th and 6th graders in Ohio, Indiana and Kentucky have either smartphones or Wi-Fi capable devices.

Sadly, the result from our survey with over 10,000, 12-18-year-old students in Ohio, Indiana and Kentucky, about 50% of parents do not manage their child's activity on these devices. Additionally, most have no idea what apps and content their kids are accessing. Nor do most understand how the misuse of technology can impact their child and their child's friends.

I often say, "No one would give the keys of a car to their 13-year-old and say, have a great night. Be back by 10:00 pm." Parents often have no issues giving smartphones and tablets to their children with no boundaries or education.

However, as we have discovered, a child can do as much damage with a smartphone to another human being as they can with a 2000 lbs. automobile.

It is for this reason, groups such as Paus were launched. Paus stands for PARENTS AGAINST UNDERAGE SMARTPHONES. The group was started by Tim Farnum, a Denver-area anesthesiologist who is proposing a ban on sales of smartphones that would be used by children younger than 13. Their website, http://www.pausamerica.com/ details many of the reason why such a ban should exist.

For example, this text greets visitors to their homepage:

"We truly are at an unprecedented crossroads in history. We all know that technology will continue to improve and play a huge part in our children's lives. What we are seeking is a balance, and we think as a nation we have gone too far. There's no reason we can't stop for a moment, and pause to consider what is best for our children."

Based on my experience, I could not agree more. However, I have found that age often has little to do with who should have access to a smartphone. Rather, maturity plays a more important part. Yet, it's hard to legislate maturity. If we did, many of us would lose our jobs.

Above all, this book is written to help our society understand the major mental health care crisis we have in our country. We can't blame smartphones, tablets and social media for every ill in America. However, we can stop and ask whether unfettered access to social media and technology might contribute to the increase in depression, anxiety and suicide ideation of our youth.

The following graphs highlight my concern.

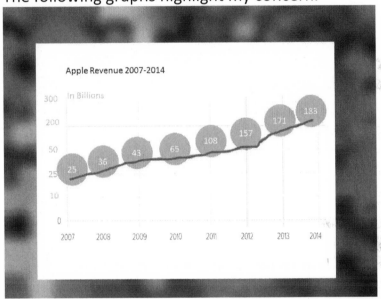

Graph one shows the revenue growth of Apple from 2008 through 2015. You see the company had unprecedented growth -- and at the time was the most valuable company in the world. Keep in mind, the iPhone was launched in late 2007 and greatly contributed to their success.

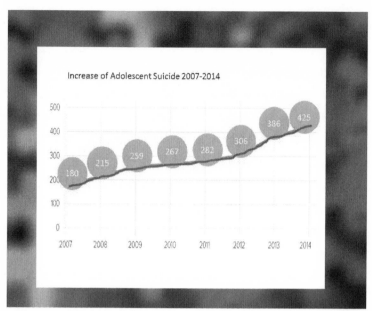

Increase of Adolescent Suicide 2007-2014

Graph two illustrates the growth of adolescent suicide from 2007 until 2014 – roughly the same time-period. Google's Android Operating System was launched in 2008 and usurped sales of iPhones significantly during that period – making smartphone technology practically ubiquitous among youth.

Are these two slides merely a coincidence? Maybe. However, I believe social media is part of the issue. So are broken families; drug and alcohol abuse; decline in family oriented media; drop in a religious or spiritual faith; a post-911 generation that has never known our country not to be at war; and the financial disaster of 2008. All of these have contributed to these systemic adolescent issues.

Every Children's Hospital in the country is struggling with these same problems. Understanding the complicated relationship it might have with technology is paramount to the health of our children. As parents, educators, grandparents, aunts, and uncles – it's incumbent on each of us to stop, look, listen and analyze the problems and search for solutions.

When reviewing the cultural landscape, subsequent to the adoption of mobile technology and social media, we have seen many unintended consequences impacting society – but in particular, our youth.

As such, this book examines the following eight subjects:

1) How We've Become A Distracted Society
2) The Trend of Sending Inappropriate Content & Its Consequences
3) How and Why Our Private Information Is Invaded
4) Stalking, Self-Esteem, and Divorce
5) Your Child and Pornography
6) Social Media & Teen Mental Health
7) Managing Your Child's Online Activity
8) Conclusion

The intent of these ensuing pages is to help us navigate the landscape of teen technology use today – and articulate what is coming down the pike in the months and years ahead.

.

Chapter 1 – A Distracted Society

One of my all-time favorite TV shows, when I was a kid, was THE ANDY GRIFFITH SHOW. In fact, years later while working in the video/film production business, our crew would often sit in our cafeteria watching reruns of the shows that we had each seen hundreds of times before. We never tired of hearing the simple yet funny banter between Barney, Andy, and Otis. Life in the 1960's seemed so simple in an era of black and white images.

I recall the episode when a visiting preacher gave a Sunday sermon related to the fast-paced world of the early 1960's.

Dr. Breen: What has become of the old-fashion ways? The simple pleasures of the past? The joy and serenity of just sitting and listening?"

I suppose to parents in the 1960's; life was fast paced. Rock & Roll was on the radio; TV dinners were in the oven and Bonanza was in color... Assuming you had a color TV.

Andy seldom had issues with Opie other than an occasional hidden turtle or frog in a shoe-box in his bedroom. Times have changed.

In real-life, perhaps every child has kept something from their parents. A note from a friend, a diary, book or magazine. Kids are curious and impulsive by nature. The desire for privacy is built into their DNA. However, as parents, it is our responsibility to manage that expectation and minimize the potential negative consequences of their online activity.

The era of paper love notes, and origami 'fortune teller' games that predicted who you would marry have faded into the ethers of the universe. They were replaced with Instagram, Snap Chat, Kik, WhatsApp, WeChat, OoVoo, Yellow, Tagged, Musical.ly, Whisper and a long-line of social media platforms that cloud each parent's horizons. It's a time consuming, arduous task to keep pace with our children while also bolstering our digital literacy.

While digital literacy should be at the top of your parental homework list, knowing *why* this is important is perhaps equally critical to successful parenting in a digital world.

To that end, we'll spend some time looking at the digital world as we know it today. Keep in mind; this world will be vastly different in 5 years. In 10 years, the world will be starkly different.

When I speak with students, I often tell them about a recent camping trip my wife and I took out west. We spent three weeks visiting Yellowstone and the Grand Tetons. Effectively we planned to lock technology away and venture back to 1976 – when we first visited these parks on our honeymoon.

What had changed in 40 years? Well, for one, we were no longer camping in a tent. Rather we were pulling a 30 foot, air-conditioned camper. My long, brown beard and hair were replaced with a close-cropped, gray beard and very little hair. My wife was the same as 40 years earlier – although she might admit to coloring her light brown locks a bit.

During our first trip, we drove a four speed, two door StarFire Hatchback without air conditioning. We listened to an AM Radio equipped with an FM Converter. We also had our trusty 8 Track for playing music by Chicago, The Beatles, Stones, Jackson Brown, Carol King and James Taylor. Life was good.

This trip, however, we were driving a large, 4x4 SUV. We had our Sirius XM radio, DVD Entertainment System, On Star, two iPhones, 2 iPads, air conditioning, two dogs and the aforementioned, thirty-foot condominium on wheels. If life was good in 1976 – life was better now. Did we live without technology for those three weeks? We did not. But we came to realize how dependent we had become on technology.

In 1976 we traveled nearly 3000 miles navigating with a road atlas and an AAA Trip Tik. Forty years later our map skills were considerably diminished by the availability of GPS and OnStar. However, to our credit, we did a great job of not checking email or doing Facebook updates. That was a modest success.

When we got to Yellowstone, it seemed like nothing

had changed. That was true for the mountains and streams. It wasn't true for the visitors.

Standing on the precipice of one great waterfall, visitors seemed more concerned with taking selfies than enjoying the wonders of God's creation.

Were families enjoying their dinners at the Lodge at the Grand Tetons – or was this the only place in the park where they had access to Wi-Fi? There were at least 100 people in a packed room – many with their noses buried in their phones, or with earbuds firmly implanted – isolating themselves from their families.

And while families still exhibited love for one another, there was no doubt that the many earbuds and Snap Chatting activity had driven a wedge between so many family members. However, this distraction is not just children.

For example, each year, the popular Highlights Magazine surveys kids ages 6–12 on what it's like to be a kid today. They publish their results in *State of the Kid.* In 2014, they focused attention on parental distraction. They discovered that 62 percent of survey respondents suggested that they feel their parents are sometimes distracted when they want to talk to them. The number one distraction? Technology.

This past year I generally would ask my teen audiences about their parent's use of technology. In almost every case, at least 50% of the teens thought that their parents were every bit as distracted by technology as themselves.

In other research published in 2014, Craig Palsson, a Yale Economist, released his findings in **That Smarts!: Smartphones and Child Injuries**.

In his abstract, Mr. Palsson writes:

From 2005 to 2012, injuries to children under five increased by 10%. Using the expansion of ATT's 3G network, I find that smartphone adoption has a causal impact on child injuries. This effect is strongest amongst children ages 0-5, but not children ages 6-10, and in activities where parental supervision matters. I put this forward as indirect evidence that this increase is due to parents being distracted while supervising children, and not due to increased participation in accident-prone activities.

As I mentioned, Palsson's study was done in 2012 when 3G was the dominant wireless connection. Today, 4G is ubiquitous as are smartphones in almost every household. Phones are smarter, 4G is faster, and parents are growing more distracted as they balance work and family schedules on a singular device that is as convenient and flexible as a Swiss Army knife on a camping trip.

According to CDC data, unintentional injuries to children under age 5 rose 10 percent between 2007 and 2012, after falling in prior decades. One must wonder if the fact that Apple released the iPhone in 2007 -- is merely a coincidence.

In another report published in the February 2016 American Psychological Association magazine, Amy Novotney reviewed a study by North Shore-LIJ Cohen Children's Medical Center. In that report, researchers observed 50 caregivers and their charges at seven different New York playgrounds. The objective: Determine how often the caregivers were distracted by smartphones.

According to the report, caregivers were distracted approximately 74 percent of the recorded 371 two-minute playground episodes. Of those distractions, electronic devices accounted for 30 percent of parental diversions. These are distractions that would not have occurred 10 years earlier

Unlike parents in past generations, who would often read the newspaper after dinner, smartphone technology is often interactive. It's immersive in ways that print on paper, or even the glow of a TV set can't emulate. Additionally, the TV or newspaper was never part of Baby Boomer's or GenX's job requirements. Today, many careers require employees to be tethered to the same device they use for their family schedules, entertainment, music, and work.

Then, of course, there is the deadly practice of texting and driving. While working at NCR in Dayton, Ohio in the 1980's I would make the daily drive from our home on the west side of Cincinnati to my office in the Far Hills suburb of Dayton. The trip was exactly 62 miles each way. At least once a week I would see a driver on I-75 reading a book or even a newspaper spread over the steering wheel during the daily commute. I recall mentioning each sighting to my wife because it seemed so unusual at the time.

In my work for A Wired Family, I drive about 33,000 miles per year visiting schools, hospitals and businesses as far north as Columbus, Ohio and as far south as Lexington, Kentucky. I am on the expressway more often than I am in my office. By my unscientific estimation, 1 in

5 drivers of cars is looking at their phones while driving 70 miles per hour. What was considered "unique distracted" driving in the 1980's has become all too commonplace in 2017?

For example, consider 2013, U.S. Cell Phone & Driving Statistics:

- In 2013, **3,154 people died** in distraction-related crashes.
- About 424,000 people were injured in crashes involving a distracted driver.
- In 2013, 10% of all drivers ages 15 to 19 involved in fatal accidents were reported to be distracted at the time of the crash.

Now consider that these stats are nearly 5 years old. Since smartphones are so much more ubiquitous today, the stats might only be worse. Regardless, these should be frightening statistics for any parents of a driving teen.

You're probably wondering, "What about that trip to Yellowstone and the Grand Tetons – and what did it have to do with distraction and technology?"

Well... I'm getting there. Perhaps the most eye-opening experience in our three-week camping trip was not the iconic beauty of the mountains; the tranquility of watching Bald Eagles soar above us while rafting the Snake River, or the frequent bear sightings near our camp. No, the biggest revelation to me was at a brief stop for a cup of coffee at McDonald's in Nebraska.

If you've ever made the trip through states such as Nebraska, you've no doubt experienced both boredom and fatigue. The long straight expanse of flatlands and corn fields tend to hypnotize you. Such was the case when we decided to stop for a cup of coffee at McDonald's which stood out like a mirage in Stephen King's, **Children of The Corn.**

Mary Beth waited in the car while I ran in for the coffee. However, when I walked through the door of the restaurant, I saw very few workers. Rather, in the lobby of the McDonalds were large, digital kiosks that had replaced the humans that once took your order. What I witnessed in the middle of corn-country was the start of what will be happening throughout our country – technology usurping jobs once done by humans. Unless you work in the food service business, you might have missed how technology is disrupting that industry. We have been distracted by our own lives and thought McDonald's would continue to provide jobs for teens and retired folks. In 10 years most of those jobs will be reduced or vanish.

It's the yin and yang of the evolution of technology. It is good and bad. Technology is developed to make life easier – but in the process, it often makes things different and more difficult. These kiosks will eventually eliminate minimum wage jobs – but will also open up new opportunities for such workers in other fields. It is a harbinger of what is to come and why education – and knowledge of technology is so important to our children.

Similarly, smartphones snuck up on all of us. In 2007 with the announcement of the iPhone, who would have thought that 4th graders would carry these into class each morning across America? Smartphones make life difficult for parents – but also allow parents, willing to understand the technology, to stay in communication with their children across thousands of miles and time zones. Times are changing at a faster pace today than ever before. The pace will not slow. It will only continue more rapidly. As parents, you must stay ahead of the curve.

That my friend is the digital landscape of today. Right, wrong or indifferent, it is the culture in which our children and grandchildren are born. We likely all feel like Dr. Breen, wishing for a more relaxed culture. Technology is not going away – nor should it. It's incumbent on us to make certain that we don't allow technology to run our families and relationships. It is there to make life easier – but we've allowed it to rule our lives and those of our children.

Don't be distracted. Be focused on the tsunami of change that is ahead.

Chapter 2 – The Consequences of Sending Inappropriate Content

Several years ago, I first heard of a new app that would allow individuals to send inappropriate messages without detection by others. The application, of course, was Snap Chat -- which was initially offered as a photo and video messaging application. To that end, users could take photos, record videos, add text and drawings, and send them to a pre-defined list of recipients. The Snap Chat user could set a time limit for how long recipients can view their video or photos — up to 10 seconds. Following that period the images would be deleted from the recipient's device.

As with so many applications in Silicon Valley – Snap Chat was developed to solve the unintended consequences of other applications. In this case, inappropriate or private photos and texts being saved or forwarded.

The genius of Snap Chat then and now lies within the minds of Evan Spiegel and Bobby Murphy. The application started as a project at Stanford University where Spiegel was a product design major. It was officially launched as a business in Spiegel's father's living room in September 2011.

What started out as a means of ephemeral communication and let's be honest -- sexting, has evolved well beyond the hope for privacy and is now valued as a $33 billion media company. Or as Spiegel claims, a camera company.

Snap Chat didn't start the trend of sexting, but it lifted into the mainstream – and made it feel safe.

But is sexting an issue among teens? The answer is – it depends on what you consider a problem.

Let's looks at the national stats.

According to Statistic Brain. 39% of teens between the ages of 13-19 have sent a sex message. Of those, 37% were girls and 40% were boys. This is an issue at many levels – but most importantly such actions are considered child pornography in most states when the sender and/or receiver are under the age of 18.

Then there is the act of actually posting such images on social media. In this case, 20% of teens between the ages of 13-19 have posted naked images on social media such as Instagram, Twitter, and Facebook.

But why do teens make such decisions? It varies – but as we know now, our prefrontal cortex is not fully developed until the mid-20. This region of the brain is responsible for planning complex cognitive behavior, personality expression, decision making, and moderating social behavior.

Then there is that darn issue of raging teen hormones. Teen hormones affect teenagers' moods, impulses as well as their body. Teen mood changes are caused by fluctuations in estrogen, progesterone, and testosterone—the sex hormones. These affect the way they think about sex.

Let's also not forget that today's media culture is flooded with half-naked images of stars who flaunt their bodies as if they're selling sleek, expensive automobiles. Only look at the Victoria Secret TV spots that appear during family television viewing and football games. Society has given its tacit approval for such behavior.

Or, consider the TV shows such as **KEEPING UP WITH THE KARDASHIANS, BIG BROTHER, and THE BACHELOR.** Each of these programs sells sex as a commodity and something that should occur on a first date.

Lastly, did I mention raging hormones?

In our October 2016 survey with teens in Ohio, Indiana, and Kentucky we discovered the following:

- 21% % of teens have sent such content to someone
- Over 50% of teens knew someone that had sent such information.

In reality, many teen boys and girls today use sexting as a means to be "fun or flirtatious." Some suggest that while they may be "virtually" aggressive using sexually suggestive words and images – that does not mean they are sexually active in "real life."

Conversely, young adults suggest that exchanging sexually suggestive content makes dating or hooking up with others more likely. This is often seen on college campuses. To that end, exchanging sexually suggestive content – especially as the teen transitions into a young adult – there can be an expectation of real sex when they meet in person.

In an October 6th, 2014 article in the Washington Post, the newspaper asked the question, "Is Sexting The New First Base?" The article was based on a 2012 study done by the Journal of Pediatrics.

Below is an excerpt:

"The findings are from within the original 2012 study, done during a six year period. A diverse group of almost 1,000 adolescents in Southeast Texas answered anonymous surveys detailing their history of sexting (or sending sexually explicit images to another person electronically), sexual activity and other behaviors. It found that one in four teens had sexted and that sexting was, in fact, related to sexual behavior."

Should parents be concerned?

Absolutely! Anyone, teen or adult sending inappropriate material should be concerned. Although I believe there are many more good people in the world than bad – it only takes one person who does not have the best interest of you or your child to ruin a life. One misguided, inappropriate photo or video in the hands of the wrong person can alter the life of anyone. That image is part of your child's digital tattoo. Once sent, your kid loses total control of that picture.

Steve Franzen, Kentucky's Campbell County Attorney,

has worked with me in his county for several years. Campbell County, although growing, is still rather rural. Whether we're talking about the inner-city of Los Angeles or a rural community in Kentucky, sexting should be a growing concern for parents.

In my recent survey that Steve completed, he said, *"Teens sharing naked photos is a common occurrence in our office, and our local police must contend with it. Unfortunately, sometimes, not always, but sometimes, we must bring criminal charges for these acts, such as the distribution of obscene material, use of a minor in a sexual performance, possession or viewing of matter portraying a sexual performance by a minor, possession of child pornography, etc. The penalty for violating these laws is extremely serious. Even adults who knowingly acquiesce in their teen's actions may be subjected to criminal liability for contributing to the delinquency of a minor or facilitating in the production, distribution, or possession of child pornography.*

Unfortunately, more than once we have had to bring charges against teens involved in videoing sex acts committed by their friends and "publishing" those acts via Snap Chat, or some other social media app. All of the juveniles involved, those engaged in the sex act, those who recorded it on their cell phone and those who posted it on social media had to be prosecuted in juvenile court."

This, of course, is not a new thing – nor one with only local implications. Neither is it simply a legal issue. Consider Amanda Todd and the many other girls who provided inappropriate images of themselves thinking that it would be kept private. Unfortunately for Amanda, it leads to constant hostility, cyber bullying and ultimately her suicide in October of 2012. The same was true for Jessica Logan, whose naked photograph that had been sent to her boyfriend, found its way to hundreds of other phones in her school and community after she broke up with him.

On July 3, 2008, Jessica returned from the funeral of a boy who had taken his life. Upon arriving home, she took her own. Her mom discovered her hanging in the closet with Jessica's cell phone on the floor nearby.

After having spoken to nearly 300,000 people on the issues of social media, the stories I hear about sexting are seldom surprising. Most of the stories are often similar and involve the sequence of steps below:

1) Girl gets boyfriend
2) Boy eventually asks for naked photo
3) Girl says no
4) Boy says he'll break up if she doesn't send the photo
5) Girl sends photo
6) Girl finally breaks up with boy
7) Boy is mad and shares the photo
8) Girl gets shamed while the image is posted on social media and shared via texting apps
9) School discovers naked picture on phones throughout the school
10) Police are called to the school, law enforcement and parents decide the consequences

About three years ago I was presenting to a small, rural Catholic high school. During the question and answer period, a freshman girl raised her hand with a comment rather than a question.

I called on her, and she said, *"Mr. Smith, you have no idea the pressure that boys put on us to send topless or naked photos. It's probably like the pressure you received in your generation to smoke. However, you knew if you smoked one cigarette it wouldn't cause cancer. However, one photo could ruin our lives."*

I remember thinking how mature it was of her to stand up and say this is front of the entire school. I also recall thinking, "If this is happening at a small, rural Catholic school, what is taking place in the large, urban public schools?"

However, the blame should not rest squarely on the shoulders of boys. We have discovered that girls are sometimes the aggressor – sending unsolicited images as a means of flirting or to attract a boyfriend.

In a recent visit to a high school, a group of first-year student boys was talking to me about social media. The issue of sending inappropriate images was mentioned by one of the young men. I noticed that as we talked, he kept looking at his phone. Since it was an informal conversation with a group of his friends I didn't think much about it. However, I asked him if the practice of sexting was an issue at his large suburban school. Without hesitation, he nodded yes and then held up his phone. Sadly, a girl had just sent him a topless photo.

We've discussed national surveys – but it's important to understand that we can't assume national surveys parallel local experiences. Sexting will vary from city to city and school to school. In our study, within a 100-mile radius of Cincinnati, Ohio we discovered that what happens in one school is often entirely different than a school just a few miles away. Teens are impacted by their peers often more than what they see and read on the web, TV and through apps.

However, sexting does happen in almost every school to some degree. It generally starts around the 6th grade. On more than one occasion I've had schools contact me to speak with students that have sent such images. In one case a bright, athletic young lady had sent a picture when she was a freshman to her then boyfriend. His dad got transferred out of town that same year, and she never saw him again. Nor did she ever make a similar mistake again.

In February of her senior year, the photo found its way to the phones of many kids in her school. She was an A student and excellent athlete. However, now that one silly photo was creating issues for a college scholarship at her dream school. She had long-forgotten about that picture four years earlier. However, technology and networks seldom forget.

In another case, a 13-year-old girl who we'll call Jill was dating a 14-year-old boy at a high school two miles from her school. Like so many young men, he asked her for a photo. She said no. He suggested he'd break up with her if she didn't. She was in love and didn't want to lose him, so she gave in.

Sadly, he immediately posted the photo to Instagram. Within 20 minutes, 20 girls at the school heard about the picture on Instagram and downloaded the image to their own devices. Within 30 minutes of Jill sending the photo, she was being bullied and shamed by 5 of those girls via text messages.

Steve Franzen provided one of the most disturbing sexting stories I've heard when I inquired about such cases in his county.

"Detectives received a report from Missing and Exploited Children regarding a 7-year-old female who had been discovered on a Twitter account which was initiated by the 7-year-old. There were videos which showed the child in various stages of undress and exposure encouraged by live viewers in Twitter and Periscope streams. The child was dancing proactively in her underwear, bra and touching herself and pointing the camera directly at her private area. The video also showed that the child was taking care of her 3 younger siblings at home while her parents were out.

One video lasted over 40 minutes where she is taking care of the children with no adult present and while she is posting videos and interacting live with viewers who made comments about her posts. The online viewers seem to be enticing her to expose herself in these videos, and the child can be heard discussing the comments made by the viewers.

In one video, the child victim appears to hold a child, change a diaper and talks about feeding the infant every day while mom is sleeping.

A search warrant was obtained and executed for the devices. A dependency, abuse and neglect petition was filed, and all children were removed from the parent's custody."

Another case in Steve's jurisdiction involved sexting on a school bus.

A juvenile, 16 years of age, participated in using his phone to videotape a sexual act that was taking place on a school bus. After finishing the taping, he proceeded to place the video on social media, which was viewed by many individuals in a span of a few hours. The principal of the high school saw the video and immediately notified the police.

The juveniles involved were picked up and received these charges:

1. *Distribution of Obscene Material to Minors – 1st Offense*
2. *Distribution of Obscene Matter One Unit of Material*
3. *Possess/View Matter Portray Sexual Performance by a Minor (1)*
4. *Promoting Sex Performance by Minor under 16 Years of Age (1)*

The cases were reviewed by the Chief Assistant Attorney, and he made the decision to send the juveniles to Court for formal proceedings in relation to these charges. When the cases were heard in court before the Judge, it was decided to send all the juveniles involved to the Court Designated Worker's Office so they could be sentenced to Diversion."

Additionally, most of us think that there is just one monolithic computer where Instagram, Facebook, and other services store your images, videos and words. However, quite the contrary. Instagram, Facebook, Twitter and other such services have hundreds of webs servers where these images are stored. That's one reason why it often takes a while for your edits and deletions to show up on these services. Additionally, there are also web servers such as Akamai that "Cache" your pages to speed up the download of your images to visitors of your social media pages.

In the case of Jill, each one of the 20 students that downloaded her image to their devices had cloud accounts. What does that mean? Simply, that when they went home that evening from school and their phones sensed the Wi-Fi in the home – those images got backed up to the cloud. Those 20 naked photos became 40 naked photos.

Given that so many colleges and employers now look at your child's social media accounts before they accept or hire applicants – having naked photos on web servers around the globe is an unforeseen consequence that this generation is just now facing.

Take for example this past Presidential campaign. You'll recall each candidate jockeying to find material from their opponent's youth that might damage their reputation. These were two, 70-year-old people that grew up in an era without millions of cell phones and social media sites capable of capturing every embarrassing action of their youth.

Today's generation will not have the luxury of their past actions hidden in the darkness of their memory. Many of their misdeeds, actions, and lapses in judgment will be captured and waiting for this generation's rise to prominence in business, education or politics. Imagine how high that bar might be in the future to secure the favor and judgment of the press, their country, and their own children.

A few years ago, <u>Lawyers.com asked famed attorney Gloria Allred</u> to provide some legal perspective on teen sexting. Below are just a few issues she broached:

- *Teens participating in "sexting" activities – those that send and receive the sexually explicit photos – are at risk of potential criminal charges for child pornography OR criminal use of a communication device, and in some states, face the exposure of having to register as a sex offender – a stigma that could haunt them the rest of their lives*
- *If a parent knows that his/her minor is engaging in "sexting" activities and does nothing to prevent it, that parent is at risk of being charged criminally with contributing to the delinquency of a minor.*
- *In addition, the parents of a "sexting" minor might have to pay monetary damages to the recipient then if it is found that the parents were negligent in supervising their child and/or failed to adequately discipline their child after the discovery that their child was engaged in "sexting."*

As you can see, parents seldom consider what their own liability might be should their child be involved in such actions.

Recently, I asked several prosecutors in Ohio and Kentucky to provide their opinion on how parents should handle sexting. Dotty Smith, Chief Assistant Prosecutor, Municipal/Juvenile Divisions of the Clermont County Prosecutor's Office said the following:

"Parents need to talk to their children about their preference. It is important that the parent/child do not download the image or send it on (as those actions are

crimes). The preference is that those kids treat unsolicited pictures/message like their parents would treat junk mail. Throw it away/delete it.

However, if the child/parent is concerned about the safety of the individual depicted in the image, the police should be notified. Again, the parent/child should not download or send the image. Place the electronic device into airplane mode and take it to the school resource officer or police station to report the concerns.

Many parents/children are concerned they will be arrested. However, in our county, we prosecute the malicious act or illegal actions, we do not prosecute the innocent individuals who are simply bringing the crime to the attention to the authorities. Every action taken on an electronic device leaves an electronic footprint, the police will be able to determine who engaged in illegal or malicious behavior regarding that image and who simply received the junk mail."

Steve Franzen, Kentucky's Campbell County Attorney, said:

"We advise the recipients of such images to contact their local police authorities promptly. The Police in Campbell County are all too familiar with this type of scenario and are more than capable of investigating and handling these activities. Not every instance will result in charges, but every instance will be investigated. Whether criminal charges will be brought is "fact specific" and made on a case by case basis, i.e., the age of the participants, their history with this type of behavior, frequency, etc."

Since many of our readers are not living in Ohio,

Indiana, and Kentucky, I'd like to provide my own perspective on how parents should handle such situations should they arise. However, before I continue, allow me to make a disclaimer. I am not an attorney, nor am I offering legal advice. You should always contact a legal authority in your state before pursuing such issues.

That said, I have had the great privilege of having talked to many prosecutors, police officers, school counselors, psychiatrist, psychologists, principals, parents, grandparents and children concerning this issue. To date, almost 300,000 people have heard our presentations. Many of them have told us their own stories.

Having lived in the media and technology business most of my adult life – and now having worked with so many schools on social media issues – I feel uniquely qualified to at least offer some advice.

With that disclaimer and background information in mind, I suggest you consider the following should your child receive a naked photo of someone under the age of 18:

- Talk with your child about the situation. Ask if they forwarded the photo to anyone. If they did, understand that they could be charged with distribution of child pornography. Discover as much as you can about the situation. As many people in the mental health and legal fields will tell you, this can have a tremendous psychological and legal impact on your child.
- Depending on the state and your school, there could be mandatory reporting requirements, which

might require you to inform law enforcement. Although most states will work with you, others could make the situation more daunting for you and your child.

- In some counties, although not mandatory, it is suggested that you report the photo to your local police. However, you must also be realistic about the long and short-term consequences. For this reason, I suggest you consider speaking first with the other child's parents. However, if a naked photo was sent or distributed with the intent to harm your child, I recommend talking with law enforcement immediately and perhaps seek legal counsel for your child. You know your child best. If you feel this will make issues worse, weigh your decision against your child's state of mind. This can have a tremendous impact on their school life and emotions.

- If your children have received any nude pictures on their phones, it is suggested that they delete the image. Keep in mind, even when deleted, the image still exists on the device. However, you and your child do not want the potential legal consequences related to possession of child pornography. Make sure a copy of that image is NOT stored on another device or in one of your cloud accounts.

- Given the rise in teen depression over the past ten years, I also suggest that you seek help from a counselor or therapist for your child.

Regardless of whether the consequences are moral,

legal or emotional -- mistakes today will live forever. And forever is a very long time.

Sextortion & The Cobra Effect

During the era of British rule in India, the government was concerned about the growing cobra population. To eliminate the serpents, the government offered a bounty for every dead cobra that would be brought to their offices. At first, the plan seemed to work. However, humans being human, an industry was born as stealth cobra breeding farms were launched to leverage the bounty for profit.

The government learned of the scam and eventually shut down the program. Those that had capitalized on the bounty were now stuck with hundreds if not thousands of venomous serpents. Rather than continue feeding them, they turned the snakes back to the wild. The result: India's cobra population actually increased.

In some ways, the technology that has developed to make some aspect of life easier or more efficient is similar. Today's apps have spawned their own Cobra Effect. Technology that allows you to take a photo and immediately send it to your friend can be used to humiliate others when posted to social media, and it goes viral

The same technology that allows a soldier in Afghanistan to see his newborn child via Skype can be used by ne'er-do-wells to extort money or favors from unsuspecting, naïve teens – a practice known as sextortion.

We have heard a lot about credit scams, whereby bank and retailer accounts are hacked and ID's stolen.

However, those financial issues are eventually, albeit often painfully restored. The issue surrounding scams such as Sextortion sometimes become permanent.

THE SEXTORTION TREND

Today there are "extortionist" that trick their unsuspecting prey into performing sexual acts via apps such as Skype, FaceTime, Oovoo and others — all the while recording the acts without the knowledge of the victim. Once the recording is complete, the perpetrator informs the victim of the video or photos and demands ransom in the form of sexual favors or money. A study on this trend was recently published in a report by Trend Micro.

The trend exists in the United States and Canada with such cases as that of James Abrahams, who hacked into the webcam and hard drive of Miss Teen USA and many other women around the country – searching for inappropriate images – and then demanding more pictures or money.

Or, consider the high school dropout Tremaine Hutchinson, who spent his unemployed days stalking young girls on Tagged.com. Once he earned their trust, he'd lure girls to send naked photos. Once the pictures were sent – the extortion threats would begin. "Send me more photos, ' or I'll send these images to everyone in your contact list."

Eventually, one of the girls was so disgusted by his threats to kill her and her parents that she told her father – who in turn called the police. Mr. Hutchinson was eventually apprehended and is now serving time in prison.

Although the threat continues here in the United States, it is of epic proportion in Asia. The Trend Micro Report details how the brains behind these attacks seduce their victims who eventually pay significant fees to keep their videos and photos from going viral. One Asian group extorted $29,204 from 22 victims before law enforcement caught up with them and uncovered a very sophisticated strategy to find potential prey and the use of malware technology.

Although these scams have not yet grown to the epic proportion in the US and Canada, we must understand that such threats do exist. With the growth of Facebook Live, Meerkat, Periscope and YouNow, extortionist have yet another tool in their arsenal to lure unsuspecting teens and adults to do things they might otherwise not consider.

THIS IS NOT NEW

In 2012, Amanda Todd became one of the first widely known victims of sextortion. She was only 14 and had unfettered access to her laptop in her bedroom. Amanda used several websites and platforms such as Facebook, YouTube, and web-camera chat sites. She met what she thought was a nice young man who showed interest in her. Sadly, like so many other victims, he groomed her over time and convinced her to send a topless photo.

Sadly, her life spun out of control as he threatened to send the image to her parents, teachers, and friends. She eventually succumbed to suicide after two years of threats by this man – in addition to physical abuse and cyberbullying by her peers.

Nearly nine years later, Dutch law enforcement arrested Aydin Coban, 35, for his alleged extortion of Amanda and many other teen girls and adult men, in Canada, the United States, Britain and the Netherlands. However, it's unknown how many other victims have gone unnoticed. Mr. Coban continues to claim his innocence.

THE DARK WEB

In a USA TODAY interview, Amanda's mother, Carol Todd said, "In the back of my mind, I never thought of a predator, I thought the person who wanted the pictures was an older teen. I never thought it was a 35-year-old man on the other end."

In reality, that's one of the greatest issues we face with our teens. We never really know who is at the other end of the communication. Moreover, it's difficult to gauge their intention or motivation. Amanda was looking for a friend and confidante – someone she could trust. Aydin Coban purportedly was looking for pleasure and self-gratification. Each chose a technology that was developed to make life easier, more efficient and pleasant.

Amanda is no longer on the face of the earth. Mr. Coban is in jail awaiting his trial. Neither was the consequence each was hoping for. Had they both only known?

ART REFLECTS LIFE

In the battle for content between, Netflix, Hulu, and Amazon Prime, there has been a wealth of original and niche programming that would not exist if not for such streaming services and the public's insatiable appetite for content.   Recently, Netflix original series Black *Mirror unraveled the subject of sextortion with the production of* "Shut Up and Dance,"

In that episode, the program illustrated some unrealistic scenarios – yet the technology behind the subject is very much real. Moreover, as we detail in our social media presentations: YOUR DIGITAL TATTOO, never before in history has it been so easy to talk, record and dupe our children into doing the unthinkable.

Does this mean our kids are bad people – and we're horrible excuses for parents? No. But it does mean that families need to be more aware of how technology can infiltrate our lives without our knowledge.

Just doing a simple Google search on the subject of "sextortion news," you'll receive over 16,000 articles on the subject. Expand the search to "sextortion," and Google returns over 356,000 links on the subject. Yet, the issue and threat are generally swept under the carpet in our homes.

To explore this sad and sadistic form of online abuse, The University of New Hampshire Crimes Against Children Research Center partnered with non-profit THORN to study the impact of this abuse.

The study discovered that women are the primary targets, and more than 50% of these victims knew the offender before the harassment began. Moreover, almost all were under 18 when the abuse started.

However, it also occurs with older teens and young adults as is detailed by ABC News regarding two George Mason University students that fell victim to sextortion, after they were blackmailed with explicit videos.

Additionally, a recent Microsoft sponsored study shows that teen sextortion is escalating, with 44% of teen respondents suggesting they experienced sexual threats or knew of instances among family and friends.

One-third of those suggesting they experienced sextortion responded that these acts occurred nearly every time they go online.

Due to the results of this study, Microsoft released some of the results early to warn parents of the online dangers. Jacqueline Beauchere Microsoft's Chief Online Safety Officer said, *"We've chosen to make this preliminary release, featuring data about teens in the back-to-school time frame to remind young people about the need for smart, safe and respectful online habits at home, at school and on the go. We will follow with an early look at key data from the adult respondents in the weeks ahead."*

As we mention in each of our presentations, please understand that there should be no assumed privacy in the digital world. Almost every app has the ability to record the communication between all parties. However, generally, the majority of the times that sextortion occurs is not a result of a hack or poor privacy settings on an individual app. Rather, sextortion usually occurs as a result of someone sharing a word, photo or video with a trusted friend or romantic partner. When the relationship ends, the offended party seeks revenge and provides the intimate results of that former romance with the world.

This happens to the best of people and their families – and it can happen to your family as well.

Please talk with your children and help them

understand that in a world of digital devices – their words, photos, and videos can cause their young lives to spins out of control. Forewarned is forearmed.

Chapter 3 – How and Why Our Private Information Is Invaded

"You are the product"

Recently, I likely became the last person on earth to convert to Windows 10. It's not that I haven't tried. In fact, on two occasions I tempted fate and transitioned our three-year-old desk top to Windows 10 – only to discover that my system crashed each time. Try as I might, our trusty ASUS desktop would have none of it.

However, my work laptop was quite another story. During our recent technology refresh, I was issued a brand-spanking new HP laptop running Windows 10. I love it. It's smart, fast and easy to learn. Although it has this obnoxious assistant, Cortana, who seems to be always stalking me – I've learned to live with her, or him or whatever.

The system is also quite inquisitive -- always asking for

information under the pretense of being service-oriented. Why all the questions? Unlike the guidance given in the movie **The Graduate**, the answer is not "Plastics." Rather, the answer is, "data."

But Microsoft is hardly the lone wolf roaming the digital plains. No, every application and social media platform lives, breathes and relies on data for its existence. We live in the economy of free.

Not really.

There is a price for everything that we do on an app. As a wise man once said, "If it's free, you are the product." Although this is true – it does not mean that paid services won't "borrow" your data. For example, I've never received a free product from Amazon, but they likely know more about me than my wife. They have my data. Data is power.

However, you get the point. We are always exchanging our private information in return for the use of an app or service, or simply for convenience. There is a cost for providing free email, operating systems, and open access to friends and free search engines. The business model requires the collection, analysis, and sale of your data.

Data Versus Metadata

I know, you've heard me use the term data and metadata. Are they interchangeable? Not really. In fact, there is an important differentiator.

Metadata is the data that defines the data. For example. You take a picture with your phone. Behind that picture is metadata that includes the size of the file; the time in which it was taken; the luminance and saturation of the photo; the shutter speed and F-Stop and often the location in which you were standing. You can learn a lot by just viewing the metadata through a metadata reader.

So, without even seeing the photo, you might know where the person was when taking the picture and at what time. You'll also know the model of the phone. You can imagine how many crimes are solved just by seeing the metadata.

Data on the other hand usually refers to the physical content of a file. In our picture example, the physical image would contain the data. What was once a beautiful landscape is converted into a binary form of 0's and 1"s to create a picture that the human eye can see.

If it were a Word document, real words are converted to 0's and 1's and then, through an application, you can view the content. That is the data.

The date, time, word count, etc., is the metadata.

Such metadata makes it easy for us to find data. It also helps law enforcement find people.

Let's say a robbery occurred at Eden Park in Cincinnati, Ohio. A suspect is caught the next day, and his phone is confiscated. The suspect swears he was not at Eden Park the evening of the robbery. His phone is inspected, and there are no photos from that day. However, there are text messages and phone calls that were made at the time of the crime.

By looking at the phone records, text messages, and other information, a treasure trove of metadata will reveal that the suspect was indeed at Eden Park at the time of the crime.

Although there is no photographic evidence —

metadata paints a precise picture of the time and whereabouts of the suspect – including any phone numbers he called, websites he's visited or to whom he sent a text message. In short, metadata is data about data.

Tag a photo: That is metadata.

Create a category for music as "country" -- That is metadata.

Click a "hate" emoji about this book: That is sad – but it is also metadata.

Write an editorial about this book: That is data.

DATA STALKERS

Regardless of what you're doing on Facebook or your child does on Snap Chat or Instagram -- or other apps, every move you make is being monitored, analyzed and then bundled with others for sale.

Let's say you traveled from San Francisco via Delta Airlines to Cincinnati, Ohio for a business meeting. When you arrive at the Cincinnatian Hotel, you log in to their Wi-Fi. You collapse on the bed and check your Facebook feed. You see a picture of your sister's baby, and you click a LOVE emoji.

You scroll down and read a link about your least favorite politician. You click an angry emoji. Later, you read an article about the newest SUV to hit the market.

You scroll through your TV GUIDE App and browse what shows are on network and cable TV. You click a few to expand the show's information. You read about **Game of Thrones, VEEP,** and **Silicon Valley.**

Before you shower, for dinner, you browse through

ESPN.com to check the scores – and later view several other sites related to music, camping, and craft beer.

Following your shower, you access your UBER app for a ride to Cincinnati's OVER THE RHINE district. You visit friends at THE ROOK and REVEL OTR before heading to the Reds' game at Great American Ballpark on the Cincinnati Bell Connector Street Car.

You finish the night with a quick beer at the Lager House before grabbing another UBER ride to your hotel, so that you are fresh for the morning meeting.

Sounds like a good evening. Other than your friends, the Uber driver, your waiters, and bartenders – few know you or anything about your travels for the day. In reality, everything you did was captured by either your smartphone, apps or all of the above.

When metadata is aggregated and analyzed, marketers know where you live and where you travel. In our scenario, they know you like craft beer and SUVs. Based on your browsing of TV shows, they know your entertainment preferences and age – and other demographic information.

They know that you are likely close to your family because you clicked the LOVE emoji of your sister's baby.

They know your politics because of the hate emoji you clicked when reading a political article.

They know you probably like camping, music and craft beer due to the various websites you visited.

Given that you visited friends in Cincinnati's Over the Rhine, they know you're likely somewhat trendy – and also a baseball fan based on your trip to see the Reds play.

Each metadata that is captured, on its own, is

practically useless. However, when aggregated together, you have a multi-dimensional picture of who you are. There is a real financial value when millions of people's metadata, with similar demographics, are bundled and sold to data brokers. That is why data and metadata are so necessary. This is why understanding the various means given to protect your private information is so important.

Still not convinced?

Let's take a look at one popular teen app: Instagram.

Last year, attorney Adam Remsem, in a PetaPixel article, examined the Terms of Use Agreement for Instagram. Let's face it, few if anyone takes the time to read such legal jargon and any explanation would be helpful. He goes into great detail as to what we give up when we click, "I agree" to their terms of service agreement. I recommend you read his article.

Yet simply reading the first paragraph of Instagram's Terms of Use should be cause for alarm:

"Instagram does not claim ownership of any Content that you post on or through the Service. Instead, you hereby grant to Instagram a non-exclusive, fully paid and royalty-free, transferable, sub-licensable, worldwide license to use the Content that you post on or through the Service, subject to the Service's Privacy Policy, available here http://instagram.com/legal/privacy/, including but not limited to sections 3 ("Sharing of Your Information"), 4 ("How We Store Your Information"), and 5 ("Your Choices About Your Information"). You can choose who can view your Content and activities, including your photos, as described in the Privacy Policy."

You might pay particular attention to the words, *"you hereby grant to Instagram a non-exclusive, fully paid and royalty-free, transferable, sub-licensable, worldwide license to use the Content that you post on or through the Service..."*

Snap Chat is similar. For example, in their Terms of Use, **"Rights You Grant Us"** section they provide the following:

*"Many of our Services let you create, upload, post, send, receive, and store content. When you do that, you retain whatever ownership rights in that content you had to begin with. **But you grant us a license to use that content. How broad that license depends on which Services you use and the Settings you have selected."***

What? I thought everything disappeared?

Those are just a few of the things we give up when we use Instagram or Snap Chat. But let's not be too difficult on those apps – others such as Facebook (which owns Instagram) Musical.ly, Live.ly, WhatApps, Tinder, Yellow and every other free app tend to demand similar things from its users.

This might not seem important to you now. But what if your child's spring break photo that was posted on Instagram becomes the promotion for Girls Gone Wild 2018? Will that happen? Probably not. Could it happen? Absolutely.

YOU'VE GONE VIRAL

Several years ago, that realization occurred to Caitlin Seida, who retold her story in a Salon article titled My Embarrassing Picture Went Viral.

According to Seida, she decided to dress up like female superhero Laura Croft for Halloween. Ms. Seida has a medical condition that has made her overweight most of her life. However, being confident in her own skin, she threw caution to the wind and went out and celebrated Halloween like thousands of others.

Following the party, she posted a picture of herself on Facebook – which by her own admission was not flattering. What resulted was a tsunami of negative comments aimed at body shaming her.

Seida said, *"So I laughed it all off at first — but then, I read the comments. What a waste of space " read one. Another: "Heifers like her should be put down." Yet another said I should just kill myself "and spare everyone's eyes." Hundreds of hateful messages, most of them saying that I was a worthless human being and shaming me for having the audacity to go in public dressed as a sexy video game character. How dare I dress up and have a good time!"*

Sadly, these are the types of character assassination you'd expect to read on a teen's post – not an adult. However, her feelings were likely much like that of a teen who had just experienced the wrath of the Queen Bees of the school.

She went on to describe her feelings, *"We all know the awful humiliation of a person laughing at you. But that feeling increases tenfold when it seems like everyone is laughing at you. Scrolling through the comments, the world imploded — and took my heart with it."*

As she readily admits in the article, she failed to set her security settings to private. That meant anyone wishing to look would have access to her picture. However, similar to Instagram, Facebook could have provided the picture to any of its partners for any purpose -- causing just as much body shaming – perhaps more. Would Facebook attempt to body shame Seida? Absolutely not! But how do they know how the images they share with their partners will be used? They don't. But their Terms of Use Agreement gives little indication how, when, where and what they might do to any image, video or word that you post.

ARE YOU A DINOSAUR OR A CROCODILE?

Last year I was speaking with my wife Mary Beth about her 34 years in the field of education. She joked and laughed about being a dinosaur. I responded by saying, "Sweetheart, you're not a dinosaur, you're a crocodile. The dinosaurs are all gone – but crocodiles learned how to survive. So have you."

In my own inarticulate way, I was trying to compliment Mary Beth for her relentless pursuit of educating students. Few if any teachers have had the impact on their students as she had over the years. She exudes a passion for educating and protecting her students. Sadly, today's children and their families are attacked from multiple directions in the form of technology, media, and culture. Often overlooked is the issue of privacy.

PRIVACY: THE CARBON MONOXIDE OF THE INTERNET

Privacy is the stealth attacker. It is seldom seen or heard. It's the carbon monoxide of the Internet era.

I often ask students or parents attending our presentation on social media, "What if after 911, President Bush mandated that every American be injected with a chip that followed their every movement, conversation, and location? How would you have responded?"

The answer, of course, is with great indignation and rage. However, the government didn't exercise such plans – nor would they need to.

A few years later, our adoption of the smart phone made the issue a moot point. Today, most Americans are as attached to their devices as they are to their limbs. It's the first thing they see in the morning and the last thing they see at night.

Americans depend on smart phones to wake them, entertain them, direct them, answer perplexing questions and -- yes at times -- speak to them. All of this happened following the introduction of the iPhone in 2007.

The physical and psychological price we have paid for such addictions include neck and back problems, hand and elbow issues, poor eye-sight, and of course that permanent stooped downward stare that seems a benchmark of every connected youth. Yet, we seldom stop to consider the privacy issues technology has brought upon us that don't involve the government or marketing companies.

In 2015, the extramarital affair site Ashley Madison was hacked, and the private information of its members threatened to be released if the location was not shut down.

Troy Hunt, who runs the site "Have I Been Pwned?", revealed the Ashley Madison site flaw on Monday, July 20th, 2015. A weakness in the site exploited its email database which allowed hackers to determine if someone may have registered for an account on the site.

What is the result for many American spouses? Well…
as Ricky Ricardo often said to Lucy, "You've got a lot of
splaining to do!"

DATA BREACHES

You would think by now that most of us would
understand that there is no guarantee of privacy in a
world dominated by technology and interconnected
digital infrastructure. In fact, approximately 50 data
breaches of prominent companies or apps are listed on
"Have I Been Pwned?". Many of us use these
resources daily, including Adobe, Snap Chat, Forbes,
Yahoo, Domino's, Sony, Vodafone and Minecraft Pocket
Edition.

Does this mean that every cretin, thief, thug, and
miscreant are attempting to secure your information or
that of your child? Of course not. But it does mean that
you, your child and your information are easier to track
than you might think. Once that information is obtained
— including just an email address – sites such as Spokeo
can track all of your public social media accounts, home
ownership information and much more for a few dollars
per month.

PRIVACY AT WORK?

Those working at large companies understand that
often corporate Human Resources departments might
monitor them through key cards and video cameras.
Additionally, the infrastructure provided by corporate IT
registers each login of laptops or tablets — including
keystrokes, email, and web browsing.

However, whether in the home, at the office or
otherwise, if you're using a corporate device --

understand that you might be under the watchful eye of HR.

THE CASE OF DAREK KITLINSKI

The same might be true for those working for our federal government.

Take the case of Darek Kitlinski, who claims that he was refused a transfer within the DEA due to his status as a Coast Guard reservist. Friction grew between him and his superior over the issue.

According to reporter Lee Ross of Fox News, after leaving a secure DEA garage, Darek noticed a red blinking light coming from under the hood of his SUV. He reached in and pulled out a still functioning Blackberry bearing a DEA identification sticker. The device allegedly traced back to the DEA's top Human Resources officer.

While these are unusual situations, it's important to note that the world of communication has changed and will continue to alter the methods we use to communicate private information.

Given the abilities of today's smartphones to record video and audio – and track location, imagine the consequences when they are used against individuals who think the information is private.

Below are just a couple of real-life scenarios that appeared in the news:

- A student confronts a teacher who had sexually abused her. Their phone conversation is recorded on her smartphone.
- A journalist records her false confessions to various priests and then broadcasts them.
- A worker is fired, and the meeting with HR is

recorded.

- During an athletic practice, a <u>coach is recorded verbally disciplining a player.</u>
- <u>Recording in a locker room when athletes are showering and changing.</u>
- <u>Recording of a conversation between doctors and nurses during surgery.</u>
- Snap Chatting by a surgeon during a breast augmentation of a patient.

WHEN YOU CLICK SEND

So, you might be thinking, this is all very interesting, but I need something with more meat. This won't happen to my kid. Right?

Well first, let me take you back a few decades. For centuries, there were few things more riveting or intimate than actual words, handwritten from the heart — to be read on paper. That's why so many of us can relate to the words of *'The Letter'* famously sung by one of my favorite singers Joe Cocker.'

It's hard to imagine old Joe singing:

Gimme a ticket for an airplane
Ain't got time to take a fast train
Lonely days are gone, I'm a-going' home
My baby just sent me a text

The art of writing and the experience of finding in your mailbox, hand-written words of love and concern have long-since vanished. Moreover, so should the thought that today's words of love and concern expressed via a digital device using 140 characters be private? There is likely no turning back the clock. Texting is often the new love letters of this generation. However, unlike 20 years ago, there is little means of controlling their distribution. Once your child clicks *send,* they have lost total control of their words, photos, and videos. Even the emoji's they click are recorded.

Your Child & Marketing Data

Although we spend significant time worrying about our kids' involvement in sexting, bullying, ephemeral digital messages, and pornography – there should be equal concern about their privacy. Why? Because they lack control over their content and the metadata that is collected by the apps they use to send their messages, pictures, and videos.

There's an entire industry that is trying to sell and buy our information. Much of this analysis of our data is done with the intent of marketing products to us based on their knowledge of our real interests. Sometimes that makes our life easier. Many times I have purchased books from Amazon based on their understanding of my likes and dislikes. However, as we have seen all too often following the Target, Home Depot and Sony hacks – there is no guarantee that our most intimate and private information will not be distributed to others and to the world.

Our challenge as individuals, businesses and a nation is to enjoy the conveniences of our digital lives while mitigating the risk of this data being unwittingly or purposely distributed. The adoption of the PC by businesses and consumers in the 1980's and then of the web in the 1990's seemed like an excellent migration to a faster and better world of communication. Few of us saw the unintended consequences of communicating on a global digital network. Moreover, who thought that this system and even smaller devices would be navigated by children in the 3rd and 4th grade – with many establishing online personas often without adult supervision? Certainly not me.

Just like a criminal on any number of the CSI TV shows, we leave evidence of our life when we use a digital device. If you're online, you are giving up a little piece of who you are. It starts out rather small – for example, the IP address of your device – but grows larger as you surf the web; fill out online forms; download apps; search words or any other activity. In that way, it's much like a detective gathering evidence. It starts with something small; but as more evidence is collected, it allows the person or system analyzing the data or metadata to construct a complete picture of who you are; where you go; and with whom you associate.

This information can be used by individual companies – or sold to third party organizations. While that might seem like a small price to pay to have access to such robust apps like Google, YouTube Crashlands, Minecraft, and others – what happens when that information is compromised through hacking?

COOKIES

Most of us have heard of those tiny pieces of digital code called cookies. They have been around since the early 1990's. They're one of those little annoyances of our digital life. How do they work? Well, when you visit many websites, they'll often place cookies related to your visit on your hard drive. These seemingly innocent pieces of code might include information related to your login or registration identification, user preferences, online "shopping cart" information, and so on.

Sometimes the info is there only to make the page load faster, or to make it easier for you to find information of interest. But as I mentioned earlier, sometimes this data is sold to third-parties. This is why that new fishing rod you viewed on the Pro-Bass website seems to follow you on ESPN, the New York Times and San Francisco Chronicle websites.

You might also know that over time the collection of such cookies slows down the processing of the device. When this happens, <u>go to your mobile or laptop settings and delete these annoying – yet sometimes helpful pieces of code.</u>

Metadata, data, and your mobile device

You might think using a mobile device makes it easier to secure your privacy. However, you'd be wrong. With mobile devices, we use apps rather than simply surfing the web. Apps often collect significant amounts of private information and send such data to the app-developer and even to third parties. This applies especially to the so called FREE apps.

What metadata might be collected by an app? Well, you might be surprised:

- Your call logs
- Your location
- Your personal contacts
- Your Calendar Information
- Your internet data
- Your unique IDs
- Information about how you use the app itself

email

Maybe you're the kind of person that believes that technology has corrupted an entire generation – and life was better in the 1980's. Hey! There's nothing wrong with the 1980's other than the music and all of that big hair. The reality is that the era of big hair ushered in the ubiquitous corporate use of email.

As consumers began to adopt the web in the 1990's email grew precipitously. Perhaps you remember those now famous words from your first AOL account, **You've Got Mail.** That first AOL account allowed us to send messages across the world to our most dear friends, relatives and perhaps our mortal enemies. They even made a movie about it by the same name. What could go wrong here?

Well, we know that answer. General David Petraeus had his Gmail hacked revealing an affair that brought his once heralded career to a stunning end.

The Sony hack revealed thousands of personal and business emails that subsequently brought to a halt the distribution of a multi-million dollar movie titled, *The Interview*. Eventually, Sony released the movie to about 300 theaters on December 23rd in 2014. In a somewhat unique twist, the movie was also available to users of Google Play, Xbox Video, and YouTube before the end of that month.

And of course, there was the Hillary Clinton email scandal of 2016.

Most of us know that when we correspond through email, we are giving information to the recipient that can be used to support or destroy us. However, you might *also* be providing information to any number of people, including your employer, the government, your e-mail provider, and anyone to whom your recipient chooses to share the message. An unencrypted e-mail message can potentially be seen by anyone while that communication is in transit. If sent from an employer-owned device, it could be read by your employer.

If you use a webmail service such as Gmail or Yahoo, your emails could be scanned by the webmail provider. This is done to both sort and detect spam and to better deliver appropriate ads to your account.

For example, Gmail scans incoming emails and places relevant advertisements next to the e-mail. Yahoo Mail performs different but somewhat similar scanning of email content.

Today's reality is that we need to be aware of the risks involved in any communication using a digital device and network.

Your Child's Apps

Apps often share your information with the developer of the app – including your general location. Be aware that a FREE app might be free for a reason. Read the "Terms of Use" and "Privacy Policy" before downloading any app to your device.

Personal information on your social media sites is accessed by search engines such as Google and Bing. The best way you keep this data and metadata from finding its way into the hands of others is to lock your security setting to **private** or **friends only**. Even then, you have no control what your friends might do with your posts

Although most adults don't use Snap Chat, Kik, Whisper, Sarahah, and other youth oriented apps – your children probably do. Each service publishes its Terms of Service that few people read when they opt-in for the app. For example, in Snap Chat's Privacy agreement they state:

"Usage Information: We collect information about your activity and the messages you send and receive through our Services. For example, we collect information such as the time, date, sender, recipient of a message, the number of messages you exchange with your friends, which friends you exchange messages with the most, and your interactions with messages (such as when you open a message or capture a screenshot). We may collect that same basic information when you use Snapcash, along with the dollar amounts sent and received.

Information Collected by Cookies and Other Tracking Technologies: Like most online services, we use cookies, web beacons, and other technologies. Cookies are small data files stored on your hard drive or in device memory that store information about your use of the Services, which can, among other things, help us see which areas and features of the Services are popular and let us count visits".

There are many other items in their agreement that anyone using the service should read before using.

RETURN OF THE BOTS

Scenario: Your child is endlessly staring at the small rectangular screen – eyebrows arched as if anxiously awaiting the revelation of life's greatest mystery from the furtive party on the other side of the screen.

She giggles with delight – and then laughs loudly followed by the words, "I can't believe you said that to me!"

Concerned that some vapid juvenile delinquent just disparaged your daughter — you grab the phone to digitally break his face when you realize the aberrant offender is not a person – but rather the MAGIC EIGHT BOT. Magic Eight Bot? What?

Yep, the round black ball of our youth is now an active bot on Kik – a popular messaging app used by nearly 40% of American teens. However, Magic Eight is just one of many bots on <u>KIK</u> and other apps — with thousands more being developed and available on apps such as Facebook, Snap Chat, and others.

What exactly is a bot or Chatbot? According to Matt Schlicht, CEO of Octane AI & Founder of Chatbots Magazine, *"A chatbot is a service, powered by rules and sometimes artificial intelligence, that you interact with via a chat interface. The service could be any number of things, ranging from functional to fun, and it could live in any major chat product (Facebook Messenger, Slack, Telegram, Text Messages, etc.)."*

You probably use them a lot but only didn't know their classification name. It could be an automated weather forecast or a voice system used for ordering food online.

Alexa and Siri are bots. If you think back to your hazy, crazy days of college, you might recall AOL's Instant Messenger known as <u>SmarterChild</u>. Well, they've come a long way since SmarterChild, and they're getting smarter.

So, why do teens find them so compelling? In some respects, because this generation's preferred means of communication can be summed up in two separate words: "Mobile" and "Messaging."

Additionally, flying under the radar for most of us is the growth of Artificial Intelligence or AI. These developments and the evolution and popularity of messaging platforms, such as — Facebook Messenger, WhatsApp, WeChat, and Viber is energizing this new age of meaningful interaction with bots and chatbots.

According to eMarketer, there are — <u>1.4 billion monthly users</u> on messaging platforms each spending about <u>23 minutes and 23 seconds</u> a day chatting. For marketers that is a potential goldmine.

Just like "brick and mortar" retailers want you to spend more time in their stores – marketers want you to spend more time with bots – because it can lead to higher product sales.

Who is at the epicenter of this change? You guessed it – your child, aka Gen Z.

Consider the Stats: Collectively, the top four messaging apps that we mentioned above have more registered users, higher retention, and higher engagement than the top four social networks. Change is not happening... it already took place when we were not looking.

So, are social media apps going away? Although the trend of downloading new apps is slowing — it does not mean that Instagram, Facebook, Twitter and others are going away anytime soon. However, it does suggest that the tsunami of new apps might be a thing of the past – as more and more people are settling on the use of approximately 5 apps.

Additionally, organizations such as Facebook are at the

forefront of bot development – adding many to their platforms. VENTURE BEAT reports that Facebook developers have created more than 11,000 chatbots for its Messenger platform. The aforementioned Kik platform – which internationally is a top teen messaging app, now has over 6,000 new chatbots.

Remember, the reason apps, and now bots exist is to sell something in one of two ways.

- To **convince you** to buy a product under the auspices of providing free, helpful information

Or,

- To sell **your** information to a marketing company.

The advantage for marketing businesses and developers is that bots can circumvent App Store approval, updates, and a user's operating system. Additionally, bot development is easier to execute. Since the very profitable youth culture spends so much of their time with messaging apps – bots are often the best means of connecting with this demographic.

As Todd Dean, co-founder and chief marketing officer at the mobile-first employment solution Wirkn wrote in Venture Beat:

"Chatbots are fun and exciting today, and teens are the main barometer and the ones to watch as they engage and drive the evolution. Companies that fund chatbot development are taking notice and voting with their wallets. There is no question in my mind that chatbots are here to stay and that they will play a very big role in the future of innovation. They may just become so human-like

and ubiquitous that we don't even know they are there."

Although there are thousands of new bots embedded in apps and websites – most are rather non-threatening to your child. Yet parents and guardians must understand that with every great technology advancement there is often inappropriate content developed around such technology. We, of course, have seen this over the years with pornography. With the proliferation and easy access to Internet porn, <u>addiction has become an issue for</u> children as young as 12. Sadly, as we've seen in the past, we now see porn bots embedded in some of the apps our kids use.

Are BOTS really spewing porn to our kids? According to a <u>2014 article in Forbes</u> writer Parmy Olson said, *"These are fake, autonomous programs that more often than not, try to entice Kik's users to click on paid-for sites with flirty conversations and the promise of porn — glorified chat bots with one thing in mind.*

According to Kik, "porn bots" make up around 1% of the app's entire message volume each day, suggesting that thousands of them regularly crawl its network."

Much of bot porn is solicited through spamming. Olson also suggested, *"The spammers may be in this for the long haul because they're making good money."*

Given the vulnerability of teens and their sometimes access to their parent's credit card information – this is a potentially expensive issue for families.

Ironically, <u>ONWARD</u> is a new bot to help minimize our addictions to pornography and additions to screen time, dating apps, shopping, gambling and video games.

Naturally, most kids are not speaking with porn bots. So what bots are they using?

According to TechJunkie, the following are the best bots on the market:

- Funny Or Die
- Joke Bot
- Notifications Bot
- Zombie Invasion
- Lingio Quiz+Translate
- The Weather Channel
- Sensay

However, TechJunkie has a warning on Sensay:

"Sensay matches you up with a complete stranger to chat about anything. It can use location to find another Kik user close by or further away and is an excellent way to meet new people anonymously. The bot will not identify your username so you actually can chat about absolutely anything. Sometimes this will work in your favor, other times it actually won't!"

When they say anything... they mean anything.

So take heed Mom and Dad. Is it better that your son or daughter is being wooed or affronted by a stranger on Kik, Snap Chat, Yellow, or Instagram – or by a bot that is storing information about their likes, dislikes, location, purchases, awake time, etc.?

Remember your answer the next time your child says to her phone, "I can't believe you just said that to me."

Public Websites

We must understand that there is so much information

about you already on public websites such as the auditor of your county that provides detailed information about your home, its value; your mortgage and your county taxes.

When you combine this data and metadata with that available by searching social media, a treasure-trove of information becomes available to anyone interested in learning more about you. One such service, Spokeo, aggregates your social media data with public information available on government sites. For less than $10.00 per month, you can quickly research anyone. However, if you have all of your social media locked down to private or friends only – none of your social media information can be accessed. That is of course unless you have made comments on someone else's social media account that is not set on "private." Then, it is there for public consumption.

Additionally, any profile photo you have ever used on social media is available to be seen by anyone –even if you have the strictest privacy settings. As such, if you or your child has ever used a photo you wouldn't want your grandma or boss to see – delete it. Even the old ones.

CREDIT CARDS & YOUR METADATA

Personal information is attached to each of your credit cards – some of which have RFID chips that can be read by anyone nearby with a RFID reader. You can't keep hackers from accessing your bank's files – but you can keep your credit cards secure by using RFID Credit Card Protector sleeves. These small, lined credit card holders block RFID signals and add another layer of personal identity protection.

Digital technologies have changed the way we work, play and raise our families. For the most part – it's been a welcome evolution in our culture. But keeping track of these changes can be difficult.

Although most us will never need to deal with many of the scenarios I mentioned, our children must know that such misuse of technology among unscrupulous individuals can place obstacles to our education, careers, and relationships. No other generation in our history has had to deal with such an evolution of technology and its impact on our private lives.

In today's environment, skilled (and at times unskilled) hackers can access smartphones externally to monitor its movements and even eavesdrop on conversations.

Smartphone Hacking on Public Wi-Fi

Although there are many ways that your smartphone content might be compromised, most frequently this occurs when you use unsecured, public wi-fi. During my presentation with teens, I show a video concerning how easy it is to hack their phones through a technique called spoofing. This gets their attention since so many of them use Wi Fi at Starbucks, McDonald's, Panera Bread and many other public establishments. It's not the fault of the restaurant or coffee shop. Rather, it's the trust that teens have related to public Wi-Fi.

Just as in your home, public Wi-Fi provides what is called a SSID. This essentially is the name of the network you are about to access and login to. If you are a frequent visitor to Panera Bread, you might not know which SSID, or Wi-Fi network that is provided for customers. For example: Is it the one labeled Panera; Panera Bread,

Panera Free Wi-Fi? We don't always know.

But before we go further, understand that pedophiles and many miscreants prey on teens and tweens. THEY KNOW THEIR MARKET!

For example:

- They know over 75% of teens have smartphones
- They know teens like to gather at restaurants and coffee shops
- They know teens access free Wi Fi
- They know that about 20-30% of teens have inappropriate photos or conversations on their devices

Knowing these facts, THE BAD GUY might hang out there as well – or in the parking lot. Using the "hot spot" capability of his device, he creates a fake Wi-Fi network that looks just like that offered by the restaurant or coffee shop. When the teen decides to use the free Wi-Fi, he or she is presented with several options – all of which look legitimate. But what if they log in to the wrong Wi-Fi? The answer: All of their photos and messages are copied without any of their knowledge.

If there are inappropriate images or videos, those are often traded with other BAD GUYS or posted to child porn websites. The teen has no idea what just happened. By the way, this happens to adults as well.

What can you do to prevent this? First and foremost, never have inappropriate info on your smartphone. If you do, you are a target for such theft. However, if you can't help yourself, at least ask the manager of the establishment for the correct SSID. However, consider these statistics: According to the INTERNET WATCH

FOUNDATION, 88% of inappropriate images find their way into the hands of those for which they were not intended. How does this happen? Often through hacks.

Additionally, never do important banking using public Wi-Fi. Although you are most likely not being hacked, it's best to do these things on networks that you know are secure.

Keep your smartphone and tablet's operating system updated. By doing so, you minimize your vulnerability to such attacks.

Consider using a VPN when doing anything outside of your network. Even then it can help you circumvent privacy issues.

As Adi Sharabani, the co-founder of mobile security company Skycure told CNBC's Jennifer Schlesinger in her 2016 article: **YOUR SMARTPHONE COULD BE HACKED WITHOUT YOUR KNOWLEDGE,** *"At the end of the day, everything is hackable. What I am surprised about is that people sometimes forget that it's so easy to hack into these devices."*

As we have discovered in our own research, any Wi-Fi used at such places as airports, cafes, and restaurants can be unsecured, allowing the BAD GUY to view everything on your device while connected.

VPN's & PROXY SERVERS

OK, you've got everything locked down at home. You know all of the passwords for every device in the house. You've secured the iTunes and Google Play stores and are running every filter known to man. You're good, right?

Well... Recently, Opera, the web browser developed by Opera Software announced that it would add a free

VPN service to its latest version. This press release created a flood of questions about online privacy, VPNs and proxy servers.

What? You actually work for a living and are raising three kids who play sports, are on a dance team, and twice a week you need to drive them to tuba practice? Now you need to be even more vigilant? No worries. We got your back!

WHAT ARE VPNs

VPNs, or virtual private networks, provide an added level of security when you're surfing the web using one of the top browsers. For example: If you're using a Mac, iPhone or iPad you are probably using the default browser called Safari.

If you're using an Android device, you're probably using Chrome.

Windows laptops and desktops generally use Explorer or its newest iteration named Edge.

And still, others might be using Mozilla's Firefox or Amazon's Silk.

All could, to some extent, provide surfing privacy

BROWSER PRIVACY

Safari, Firefox and Amazon's Silk, privacy features are called, *PRIVATE BROWSING*

In Google Chrome it's called *Incognito.*

Explorer/Edge refers to this feature as *InPrivate Browsing.*

Opera not-so creatively refers to theirs as *Private Tab / Private Window.*

In essence, each attempt to provide some level of privacy from advertisers and others interested in knowing your browsing information.

But hey! You don't want anyone sniffing around your digital world without a search warrant unless they're also carrying a gift card to Starbucks. What are your options? The answer very well might be the use of a VPN or perhaps a proxy server.

OK, TELL ME MORE ABOUT VPNs

There are hundreds of VPNs from which to select. Some are free. Some charge a subscription fee. However, for this conversation, we'll address some of your free options.

As we mentioned, if you adopt the Opera browser on your laptop or desktop, you'll have a free VPN service. This allows you to surf the web without too much concern from snoopers. You can also access the foreign versions of services such as Netflix. However, this same technology also allows your child to circumvent some of the controls you've placed on your network.

For now, the service will only work on a laptop or desktop. However, future versions will be available for mobile devices.

HOLA

Firefox offers the Hola or Hola Unblocker as a free VPN service. However, I've often had issues when adding certain plugins on Firefox. Although Firefox supposedly checks each plugin that they offer, I have found them to sometimes have issues.

BETTERNET

Google's Chrome allows Hola and other VPN services

such as BetterNet. BetterNet is considered a quality service with an excellent reputation.

Both Hola and BetterNet are available for mobile devices as well.

Most VPNs provide some great features, such as:

- Perhaps one of the biggest benefits is the protection they provide when using public WiFi hotspots. These hotspots are often used by hackers searching for private data. VPNs can minimize the chance of a hacker accessing your information.
- Hiding IP addresses by masking a user's IP address with a virtual IP address. The result? It makes it more difficult for the sites you visit to track you.
- Unblocking firewalls and websites. In this case, the VPN allows users to bypass blocked sites by circumventing the network. This has been a huge issue for school networks

In essence, VPNs helps to maintain your private communication by hiding your digital sessions from the criminal elements. Or if you're a criminal, it can hide your activity from law-enforcement.

VPNs are the equivalent of placing a small hose inside a larger hose. Both hoses are streaming water in the same direction, across the same property. However, the smaller stream is shielded from mixing with the other data.

In the case of your VPN protected data, it is not easily viewed by others on the same network.

However, don't be fooled into a false sense of security when using VPNs or proxy servers. GOLD FROG wrote an excellent article a year or so ago when they did a detailed analysis of such strategies. Any of these approaches should be used only as a safeguard against your private information being stolen. However, no system is perfect. No system is impenetrable from someone that knows what they're doing.

NOW, WHAT THE HECK IS A PROXY SERVER?

Chances are if your child uses a tablet or device on a school network, they are intimately familiar with proxy servers. Proxy servers are used to evade school networks so that students can legitimately access great training videos on YouTube, or in some cases porn on other sites. A proxy server hands off a request to an authorized website by using another site's URL or address.

In such a case, the school or businesses' network filters are fooled into thinking that the requested website is acceptable. The network then delivers the unacceptable (but requested) web content to the user.

Recently, the online site, TRICK SEEK published a list of the top proxy servers available. It's an interesting read that will give you an insight into how easy it can be to hide your identity or online activity.

When dealing with your kids, the best protection against them visiting an inappropriate website is by just talking to them about your concerns. Building trust between a parent and a child is sometimes a forgotten art. However, most students with whom I've spoken want that conversation. Moreover, they want to build that trust.

However, I also have spoken to many parents that regardless of the strategies they take, their child has attempted to undermine every policy. In those cases, please consider the <u>parental controls and router</u> <u>strategies we have discussed in this book.</u>

OPERA: THE ITALIAN WORD FOR "WORK"

We started this discussion with news about the Opera browser. Interestingly, the "art" that we know as Opera is considered the fusion of music, drama, visual arts, and dance. It's also the Italian word for "work" and has a 400-year history in western civilization. It truly was an evolution in the world of the arts.

In the world of network technology, we too are seeing the development of "digital technology" as the 2017 & 2018 world of mobile apps collides with the 1995 world of websites. Somewhere in-between will be a new world for parents to master. For now, you're armed with what many of your kids already know.

It's difficult to digest and manage this change of technology. Or, as the Italians might say. *It's Opera.*

Facial Recognition

How many times have you uploaded photos to Facebook and thought, "how does this app know that pic is of weird Uncle Charlie?" Perhaps you wondered briefly and then went to the business of uploading your child's birthday party pics, or last weekend's barbecue.

However, the reality is that Facebook is using a potent tool known as <u>facial recognition software.</u> In fact, many say that Facebook's actual facial recognition program is much more robust than that used by the FBI to catch every ne'er do well from here to Helsinki.

But what if someone were able to secure every picture associated with Facebook? Other than an absolute violation of your privacy – what harm could there be? The answer might surprise you. Why? Because if anyone had access to all of the social media photos on apps such as Facebook, Instagram, Twitter, Musical.ly, Snap Chat, etc., it would mean they'd have a window into your identity – without having ever met you.

For example, Government uses facial recognition technology to catch the bad guys. However, 26 states use this same technology for everyone with a driver's license.   This allows government agencies to quickly identify you – and identify anyone that has stolen your identity.

Maybe we're ok with our federal and local governments being able to identify us under the auspices of preventing identity theft. But what about social media companies? Should they have access to such power?

As suggested, Facebook's technology is better at identifying people through photos than the FBI. This is in part because Facebook has 1.65 billion users – each of whom posts hundreds – if not thousands of pics each year. Therefore, their data sets are better and facial recognition learning becomes enhanced. This is called Machine Learning.

But can someone steal your photos on social media? Today, if a user's account does not have the proper privacy settings, these pictures can be compromised and used for just about any purpose. In fact, you cannot secure your profile picture on any social media platform. They are open to the public.

To our knowledge, no one has been able to hack Facebook's entire collection of photos and associated metadata. However, someone has been able to access a dataset containing 40,000 images of both men and women from Tinder. Given that most of these photos are not of "the big 3", i.e., birthdays, bar mitzvahs or barbecues – the stakes are little higher for those whose images grace the digital vaults of Tinder.

Stuart Colianni wrote a program to compile Tinder photos, intending to use them for machine learning research. His rationale: "Why not leverage Tinder to build a better, larger facial dataset?"

For his research, he added folders containing the photos to Google's Kaggle, a service that provides programmers the ability to experiment with artificial intelligence algorithms. Such algorithms can be focused on large photographic datasets to perform facial recognition tasks.

Well as one might imagine, this upset the folks at Tinder – but not half as much as the college students, married doctors, Lawyers, CPA's and other professionals and non-professionals whose alter-egos "were looking for love in all the wrong digital places."

So what's the big deal? In short, as was reported in a recent Vocativ article,

"... strangers can use them to catfish others — the act of posing as a person to lure another. Internet strangers can also reverse search nameless photos and potentially find who they belong to as well."

Again, it's hard to compare Tinder's User Stats to that of Facebook's 1.65 billion users. But given the perspective mentioned by Vocativ above, imagine the damage that could be inflicted on Facebook users if every such photo became part of a sophisticated, Artificial Intelligence, and facial recognition database.

We must come to grips in this generation of algorithms — that our faces are nothing more than mathematics. In fact, the math that makes up our face never changes. As such, if you have sophisticated facial recognition technology — your high school picture could be scanned and subsequently find you on any number of social media platforms, 5, 10, 30 years after you graduated.

Surprised by all of this? Most people are. However, flying under the radar for most of us is Google's "Vision" and Amazon's new Image Recognition service called "Rekognition." (Yes spelled with a K)

Amazon's service was launched in 2016 and according to their website, *"Rekognition API lets you quickly build powerful visual search and discovery into your applications. With Amazon* Rekognition*, you only pay for the images you analyze and the face metadata you store. There are no minimum fees, and there are no upfront commitments."*

Although this service won't help you hack Facebook or other social media apps, it will help you identify people in photos that you might take or have found elsewhere. There is a free tier that will help you understand how powerful facial recognition is — and where this technology might take us in the future.

Not everyone wants to pay for such services. In that case, there is reverse image look up sites such as Tin Eye that can find identical images on the web by scraping social media sites to unearth the exact images that you use for your search.

This is just the beginning.

Fortunately, the scraping of 1.65 billion user photos on Facebook did not happen this week. However, 40,000 Tinder users are wondering what disturbing images of them might be floating in the ethers of the Internet.

SOCIAL LISTENING & YOUR CHILD'S SCHOLARSHIP

A few months ago, I was visiting an Ohio high school to present our Social Media program to two different groups of high school students. While waiting for the second group to enter the auditorium, the football coach approached me and said, "I wish you had been here yesterday." I laughed and asked him, "Why?" He then went on to tell me how his number one player had just lost a $200,000 football scholarship to a Division I program for sending one negative Tweet about a girl in the school. Apparently, the young man didn't know that most Division I schools have staff that use social listening programs to monitor recruits and existing players on social media.

It used to be that the only way you could keep tabs on your recruits was from their high school coaches, school administration, the newspaper covering local sports and when allowed — periodic phone calls to the recruit. Those days have long since passed. Today, there's social listening.

Say what? Social Listening comes in a variety of forms. In some cases, it's simply a staff member in the athletic department who manually follows high school recruits and current players through their activity on Twitter, Instagram, or Facebook. For larger athletic departments, it's using such tools as GeoFeedia, SnapTrends and other tools that can literally follow hundreds or thousands of feeds from athletes on most any given social media platform. Schools that might spend $500,000 in tuitions and development of a player want to be certain the young man or woman is of good character and behavior. These tools are often part of the litmus test.

In my travels, I've likely made the same observations as you. An 18-year-old boy or girl might look like an adult, but in many ways, they are still kids. Then consider that each one of them has a tool in their hand that provides instantaneous self-gratification through ephemeral texting, heavily filtered selfies, hashtag laden tweets and sentence ending emoji. Even the best of teens often will say and do things without any thought of the consequences.

LACK OF EMPATHY MAKES COLLEGE COACHES WONDER

In her book, <u>UnSelfie, Why Empathetic Kids Succeed In Our All-About Me World,</u> Michele Borba, Ed.D., an internationally renowned consultant, educational psychologist and recipient of the National Educator Award studied this issue. She suggests that many teens are so obsessed with texting and "selfies" that they've never learned empathy for their peers and those in their homes and community.

I think all of us have been out to eat only to see a family of 4 with their noses buried in their phones without regard to the people at their table. The human social factor that helps to deliver empathy is often missing in today's youth.

The resulting "Selfie Generation" has indeed created an "empathy crisis." In her book, Dr. Borba says that teens today are *forty percent* less empathetic than they were just a generation ago, and narcissism has increased *fifty-eight* per cent. Much like the boy that lost a scholarship for sending a nasty tweet about a girl at his school – our new digital culture has led to teens making rash judgments and taking quick action without regard to consequences.

However, there are countless examples of how a teen's digital actions have created enormous obstacles to their future success. It is often best witnessed during the recruiting season at high schools across the country.

The problem continues when the recruit enrolls in the college. Assistant IU basketball coach, J.D. Campbell told the Indy Star, *"It's just really important, to be honest, and really important to remind them as much as you possibly can, that your reputation is always on the line. Break it down to them that this is your family, you represent your family first."*

Your digital reputation can follow you for life – there's no taking back a Tweet, a post, a picture or a video. If it's on social media, it's now searchable.

Nebraska director of player personnel Ryan Gunderson told ESPN that social media, *"Has revolutionized recruiting. Sure, cell phones have had a huge influence in the process, allowing recruiters to go mobile with their communication. But with today's technology, cell phones are merely a vehicle for social media use."*

Unfortunately, for every good, there is often a bad. Through social media, coaches can easily see what a recruit is posting; what they like or share; and have access to their social media friends. In just a few minutes, a coach can decide an athlete's behavior and character. It might not be the reality – but as they say, "perception is reality." You seldom have a chance to explain. In 30 seconds you could be written off of a recruiting list due to your social media activity — and not even know it.

In the ESPN January 2016 RecruitingNation Article, Jeremy Crabtree wrote about SMU Defensive Coordinator Van Malone. Coach Van Malone tweeted a redacted dossier on one of the Mustangs' commitments. It's a tremendous insight into how coaches make decisions as it relates to a recruit's social media activity.

Social media can illustrate a student's work in the community, their academic and athletic accomplishments and their communication skills. Social media has infinite possibilities for those who master its positive use.

"I wish you had been here yesterday," resonates with me still today. How many young men and women were on the radar of a college but unbeknownst to them, they were dropped from the coach's whiteboard due to their online behavior?

Social listening has made the job of recruiting a little easier for those with access to social listening tools.

With social media, character and behavior count more than ever.

To all parents, grandparents, and students out there – learn to be a crocodile... Not a dinosaur. Learn to change and manage the technology and culture before the technology and culture change you and your children.

Failure to manage your online privacy might leave you with, "A lot of splaining to do."

THE INTERNET OF THINGS (IoT)

A few years ago, I first heard of The Internet of Things, or what is more commonly referred to as IoT. Essentially, The Internet of Things is the connection of electronic devices, in homes, cars, and buildings that allow them to be controlled remotely and exchange and compare data.

Such devices could be as simple as the NEST thermostat in your home; a sensor in your car; a medical device that controls your heart rhythm; the lights in your home; a camera on your front porch; or any number of devices that can connect to a network.

What we call SmartHomes essentially allows everything in your home to talk to each other. Moreover, it can help you save hundreds if not thousands of dollars per year on utility costs by being able to automate and remotely control every device in your home.

Projections suggest that by 2020 there will be 24 billion such connected devices throughout the globe. However, since this is a "green field" industry, it can also create privacy issues.

In the next few years, more cars will be connected to the Internet – allowing them direct communication with SmartCity infrastructure. This might permit the redirection of vehicles during heavy traffic.

Doctors will be able to monitor ailing patients from their home – reducing the need for inpatient observation – thus reducing healthcare costs.

There are literally thousands of changes coming to our world due to the billions of tiny sensors embedded in everything from toasters, refrigerators, lights, traffic systems, dams, electric plants and any other aspect of infrastructure that can better serve humanity through an Internet connection.

However, like all progress, there are potential issues – the biggest of which is the impact on our privacy.

A few years ago, when wireless routers that provide Wi-Fi in our nation's homes were first released, the majority of families never changed the security settings of the router. As such, it was easy to drive down your neighborhood street and use your neighbor's Wi-Fi. Moreover, it made it easy to gain access to the devices in their homes. To a lesser extent that still occurs today.

Now imagine having 5, 10, 20, 100 devices – each with their own ID. Without proper security, it will become somewhat easy to hack your neighbor's lights, TV, thermostat and any device that is not properly secured. As the IoT becomes more ingrained in society, product developers realize the need to create easy to manage devices and controllers. However, this is still a nascent industry – and not every manufacturer of such devices is there yet.

You might be asking, "What value is there to hacking my connected devices?" The answer is, your activity on these devices is part of your private profile.

For example, you watch TV. There might be TV programs that you view that you wouldn't want your boss, neighbors or church clergy to know. Well, a group of researchers from the University of Michigan showed just how easy it is to hack a Samsung SmartThings smart home system. Such hacking could easily provide such TV viewing information – in addition to allowing ease-dropping through the connected TV's microphone and camera.

In the case of your car, imagine your driving profile including speed, location, miles driven, accelerations and hard stops being reported to your insurance company. This is already possible today through OnStar and other services. Yet you are making that conscious decision when you register for the service and subsequently request a discount from your insurer. However, would you want private detectives to have such info? What about an attorney in divorce cases? Could they gain access to your driving information in child custody cases to prove that you endanger your children?

And what about your grandfather's pacemaker? Can that be hacked? The answer is anything can be hacked given enough time, resources and knowledge. This is not to say the IoT should not move forward. It is to suggest that we didn't see the unintended consequences of the smartphone. We should learn from that mistake before we decide to connect our homes, life, and family to the Internet.

Chapter 4 - Self Esteem, Stalking, Cat fishing & Divorce

Last year I received a call from a group in England asking if one of their writers could post an article on our website. Until then, I had written every article and video on A Wired Family. Being somewhat protective of our company and the site, I asked several questions before giving it serious consideration.

The writer's representative told me that they wanted to write an article concerning the impact Instagram has on female teens and their self-esteem.

Having daughters and granddaughters, I was interested in their perspective. I agreed that we'd give them permission if the finished article met with our approval.

A week or so later, I received the article from **Lucy Whittaker**. Lucy studied psychology before traveling for 6 years in Africa and then Asia. She now writes for her local newspaper while also contributing to the family printing business.

Lucy's first two paragraphs caught my attention:

"With all the seemingly flawless women posting filtered pictures of toned bodies in bikinis and full-on makeup transformations, Instagram can be a dangerous place for young girls. A couple of years ago, an Australian then-teenager and ex-model named Essena O'Neill admitted to her unhealthy obsession with the app, and many young adults share the same sentiments. Instagram users find themselves taking 10 photos before posting a so-called candid, or deleting posts because of the lack of likes. According to THE GUARDIAN, O'Neill quit the platform, calling it "contrived perfection made to get attention." If this is how Instagram manipulates its older users, can you imagine how detrimental it is to our young daughters?

From filters to airbrushing features, girls are pressured now more than ever to look their best in the virtual world. Browsing through their feeds, they discover that those that upload pictures of their skinny beach bodies or their new skin-tight bodycon dresses are often leading in this popularity contest. It's the kind of attention people crave in the digital sphere and teaches users a terrible formula of a good Instagram post. Even all the makeup transformations are teaching young girls how to put on all these products, leading them to wear an unnecessary amount of foundation, eyeshadow and such to school every day."

Was this how young ladies really felt? Were they drawn to this app like moths to a flame – with many a similar outcome?

A May 2017 study by researcher Matt Keracher for the UK's Royal Society for Public Health seems to agree with Ms. Whittaker's assessment.

"Instagram draws young women to "compare themselves against unrealistic, largely curated, filtered and Photoshopped versions of reality,"

"Instagram easily makes girls and women feel as if their bodies aren't good enough as people add filters and edit their pictures in order for them to look 'perfect,' " an anonymous female respondent said in the report.

In fact, of the top social media apps used by teens in the study, only YouTube was deemed to have a positive impact. However, YouTube has its own set of issues.

So, let's go back to the year 2007. Steve Jobs is about to walk onto a black, spotlighted stage to reveal his latest, greatest product. As he approaches center stage wearing his black turtleneck, blue jeans, gym shoes, and John Lennon glass the crowd await his introduction with nervous anticipation. Everyone in the audience thinks that he'll be introducing several products. However, instead, he surprises most by introducing just one product that has the features and functionality of many products. That product, of course, was the iPhone.

I wasn't there, but I recall watching the playback on the web. I was as excited as anyone in the crowd. I had followed Steve Jobs while I was a writer for NCR Corporation. He and Bill Gates were the tech rock stars of my era. But as enthused as I was about the iPhone, I never in a million years would have thought that this singular device would play a role in how young women and some young men would perceive themselves.

I would have not thought that this device, would be at least in part, become a major vehicle for the growth of bullying and teen depression.

Nor did I think that lives would end on the streets and expressways of our country due to texting and driving.

Although the iPhone was not the first smartphone – it was the first smartphone for the consumer. It caught the public's fancy with little thought to the consequences. Within just a few years those first iPhones and later Google Android devices would make their way from the hands of parents to those of their children.

As I mentioned in an earlier chapter, our DIGITAL TATTO series was developed due to the unfortunate suicide of an eighteen-year-old woman. But even I, someone that had researched social media so thoroughly, had little knowledge of how profane the use of social media would grow with teens in our society until, one day while visiting a small Catholic grade school in 2009.

The building was located on a quaint, urban campus that appeared to have weathered well the advance of time over its 80 some years of existence.

The school was run by an articulate, energetic, elderly nun who greeted me with a hardy handshake and bright smile. As with any presentation, I asked her if there had been recent issues in which I should be aware. She paused and then told me that over the summer, a 7th-grade female student who I'll "Jane" had created a "fake Facebook account" in the name of another female student named "Lori" with intent to humiliate her. Jane uploaded naked photos and videos that were of another

91

similar looking young lady that could be construed to be Lori. Since Lori didn't have social media, she wasn't aware of the fake Facebook account until she returned to school. She was consequently humiliated by the page and subsequent comments made to her in school when she returned from summer vacation.

Lori's parents and the principal became aware of the site through comments made by other parents at the start of school. They quickly called the police — who in turn felt the Facebook page to be vile enough to contact the county prosecutor.

After reviewing the issue, the prosecutor requested a subpoena from a judge so that they could legally secure the IP address from Facebook of the computer that generated the original Facebook account. In time, law enforcement was able to track down Jane -- who had created the original fake account. She was summarily expelled from school and potentially faced both criminal and civil consequences for her actions.

I learned so much in those first 10 minutes of my conversation with that elderly nun – not about technology – but about the psychology and motivation of young people. She had spent her entire life working with young people. She knew kids over multiple generations. Nothing really surprised her. At the ripe old age of about 75, she had learned the "ins and outs" of children, technology, and the legal system. I was amazed.

Since that time, it appeared that issues related to teens creating fake social media accounts had all but vanished from the ether's of "The Network." However, this past year, incidents of such behavior appear to be again on the rise. This time the app of choice is Instagram.

It begs the question, when is it a crime? Perhaps more importantly, what steps can you take if it happens to you or your child?

WHEN IS IT A CRIME?

This is not an easy question to answer. What might seem obvious is not always the case. The law is evolving and interpreted in light of technology that we could never have conceived 10-20 years ago. In short, it's generally assumed to be illegal to ever provide another person's personal information with the intent to do them physical or emotional harm. But the motivation of one's actions is not always easy to prove.

Some possible illegal scenarios that we often see with teens include:

- Stalking and/or posting embarrassing or false information about an individual
- Harassing someone using digital media, websites, apps, etc.
- Logging into another person's social media account without their specific permission
- Threatening another person or using intimidation — including the threat to post something online if they don't provide something to you. This often takes the form known as "sextortion."

Are these always a crime? Not necessarily. Remember, each case is different. How each jurisdiction handles such cases will often differ as well. However, I recommend you visit RISE & STAND. They are a non-profit organization that helps individuals and organizations dealing with such issues. Again, bullying, harassment,   identity theft, extortion, and sextortion are all serious issues. Check with the proper authorities in your area before attempting to pursue legal recourse for someone's online actions against your child.

In reality, illegally using social media comes in various flavors. However, the following scenario is somewhat typical of what you might find in middle and high schools.

SCENARIO:

Jill has been best friends with Julie since the first grade. They vacationed together and have played soccer together for years. However, recently Jill has become annoyed because of the attention a boy they both like has given to Julie. Since then, they stopped sitting together at lunch and seldom talk in the hallways of their school.

The tension continued to build over the course of a month until Jill decided to get even with Julie by creating a fake Instagram page using Julie's identity. She copied several photos from Julie's real Instagram accounts and from images she screen grabbed through Snap Chat. She then posted them onto the new public Instagram page she created as Julie. She also found some inappropriate photos by doing a Google image search and posted them onto the same fake page — alluding that the girl in the inappropriate photos was Julie. She then sent out friend requests to all of Julie's friends. Many of them were surprised to have received the invites because they were already followers of Julie. However, most went ahead and accepted.

Julie's friends were shocked by the images — with many deciding to shun their long-time friend. However, a few quickly brought the issue to Julie's attention.

Julie was devastated by the Instagram page and the subsequent bullying that ensued by some of the boys and girls in her class. She told her parents of the issue who then immediately contacted the school principal. The principal contacted the school resource officer for his opinion. Given the naked images that appeared on the page — and the references to sexual behavior of a minor, the school resource officer contacted the local county prosecutor.

Upon reviewing the same information, the county prosecutor requested that a judge issue a subpoena to Instagram to reveal the IP address of the person that created the fake Instagram account under Julie's name. The judge agreed.

Since Instagram has an entire department responsible for responding to such subpoenas, Instagram turned over the records related to Julie's fake page — including the IP address of the tablet used to create the account. Law enforcement contacted Jill and her parents and eventually revealed all the evidence related to the date, time and IP address used to create the page.

Jill now has a problem:

- There is verifiable proof that her tablet was used to create this fake page. It was the same tablet used to create all of her personal social media pages. Moreover, her parents know that she has been annoyed with Julie for the past 30 days and certainly had the motive to attempt to hurt her.
- Since Jill had broken the "Responsible Use of Technology Pledge" in the school's Handbook, the school suspended Jill from class for one week.

- Julie's parents are furious. Their daughter hasn't slept well since the page was created. She endured hurtful text messages from her classmates and faced embarrassing comments in the halls of the school. Her parents are seeking a civil suit if the criminal courts don't punish Jill.
- Lastly, and perhaps the least of Jill's problems relate to her user agreement with Instagram. Jill violated multiple aspects of the Agreement by posting naked pictures; posting copyrighted material from a Google search; and by creating an account without the permission of Julie. Jill has now been suspended by Instagram.

REALITY CHECK

In an ideal world, this is how most cases would begin to unfold. The culprit would be found and quickly face the consequences of their parents, school, and the courts. However, this is not NCIS New Orleans. Seldom are crimes neatly wrapped up in 60 minutes, with a detective smugly smiling at the camera as the file is placed into the CLOSED CASE drawer.

In the real world, law enforcement must prioritize what cases should consume the time and treasure of their offices. Sadly, the growth of heroin; other street crimes and now terrorists using social media, smother already strangled police departments and court systems. If no person is severely damaged by the actions of another — Julie's parents might be forced to seek other avenues of justice; such as a civil suit or talking it out with Jill's parents and the school system.

While the above scenario involves malice on the part

of Jill, often cases involving fake identities are simply pranks. However, they're not without their consequences as well. It can be illegal to access or change someone's social media account and/or password without their permission – even as a joke. The issue grows significantly if you use their account to threaten or extort favors. But again, reality suggests not every breached account can or will be fully pursued by law enforcement. Like many things in this new technology driven world, the law does not always sync-up with reality. Always check with an attorney before pursuing such cases.

In the United States, we have what is known as the Computer Fraud and Abuse Act or CFAA. There are many areas covered in this act – but in large part, it makes it illegal to intentionally access a computer without authorization from the proper owner or management of that system. Unfortunately, the law does not explain what "without authorization" actually means.

CFAA is not to be confused with Identity Theft laws in the United States. Yet, these laws and that of CFAA each play a role in what you or your child may or may not do online. You can find more information on these issues at the website of Stay Safe Online. Their stated mission is *"To educate and empower our global digital society to use the Internet safely and securely."*

That said, often a parent feels compelled to move forward with a law suit. For example, in 2012 after her school and police said that they could do nothing about a fake Facebook page and subsequent cyber bullying, a Georgia teen filed a suit against two of her classmates for creating a fake Facebook account in her name. They distorted photos of her; posted a racist video that implied she hated African-Americans and suggested that she was sexually active and a drug user.

Cases such as this can be traced back as far as 2007 after an adult named Lori Drew created a fake Myspace account with her teen daughter and another girl to assist in bullying 13-year-old Megan Meier. Sadly, Megan later took her own life. Drew was charged and later convicted under the Computer Fraud and Abuse Act for violating Myspace's terms of service by creating a fake account. Unfortunately, the conviction was overturned by a judge.

Sharing Passwords Is Part of the Problem

Frankly, sharing smartphones and tablets happens every day at schools across the country. Often teens know each other's passwords for devices and associated accounts such as email and social media. By logging into one another's accounts and sending messages without permission, teens can face charges as well. This is particularly important to understand should a message be sent that is vulgar, threatening or contains images of a person under the age of 18 in the state of nudity or partial nudity. But remember, if you pursue this through legal channels it is not a guarantee that you'll win in criminal or civil court.

Another somewhat related story is worth noting. In 2013, in New York, there was the case of Ian Barber. Allegedly Mr. Barber posted naked photographs of his girlfriend (now ex-girlfriend) to his Twitter account. He then also sent the illicit pictures to her sister and her place of employment. Many view this as the first "Revenge Porn Case." Eventually, among other offenses, he was charged with Aggravated Harassment in the Second Degree.

Unfortunately for his ex-girlfriend, the judge dismissed all three charges. You can read more about this story in the article published in *The Atlantic,* titled, What The Law Can and Cannot Do About Online Harassment. This story illustrates how difficult it can often be to win such suits in a system whose laws don't always sync with this evolving technology. Although this scenario had nothing to do with sharing passwords – it indicates how sharing anything online can create havoc for once loving couples or friends.

However, as far back as 2011, articles concerning the practice of trusting best friends or those in a relationship have been written. In fact, that same year, Pew Research revealed that 30 percent of teenagers that regularly used social media shared a password with someone such as a friend, boyfriend or girlfriend. Girls were almost twice as likely as boys to share.

Catfishing

No, we're not talking about Hillbilly Handfishing,' the reality television show about the noble sport of fishing using only your bare hands and feet. In this case — Catfishing is related to the creation and use of fake online profiles. The reference started as a kind of Internet dating hoax made popular by the 2010 documentary film and MTV reality series. Generally, the motivation for catfishing is for the purpose of developing a misleading internet liaison. Online teens and adults might simply create a fake profile with seductive pictures or comments meant to lure in their victims. Often times the victims are individuals with low self-esteem, lonely or simply curious.

But that is not always the case.

In fact, the University of Michigan hired the company, 180 COMMUNICATIONS to help teach their football players a lesson in how they can be easily lured. The company used a beautiful young employee to send a friend request to every member of the football team. Many were all too eager to oblige. Beautiful young girl... Athletic young men playing for a high-profile university....What could go wrong?

Fortunately, nothing went wrong since the university was using this as a lesson for their players, i.e., "Don't trust that the person on the other side of the app is who they say that they are." Don't believe me? Just ask Manti Teo.

WHAT ROLE CAN SCHOOLS TAKE?

All schools throughout the United States and in most western countries consider cyber-bullying and catfishing to be a serious crime. Most schools have policies against such actions whether on the school premises or otherwise. At the start of the year, most of these institutions review this policy with their students — often requiring the parents of the student to sign the policy or handbook.

Social media has placed a heavy burden on schools to police the actions taken outside of the school. Social media often creates disruptions inside the walls and on the grounds of the school. To that end, the punishment that a school provides might be swifter than that of the court system.

For example, Students who bully other students — and in some cases bully teachers — can face suspension or expulsion. Moreover, as we mentioned, the school system might also request the opinion of the local police to determine if a crime has been committed.

What can you do to protect yourself and your children?

Below are five quick steps to consider in protecting your family against having social media accounts breached or children being bullied.

1. Always monitor your own online activity and that of your family: If you believe that your account – or the account of your child has been hacked, change your password immediately. Also, most sites have a contact link that allows you to report such suspicious activity.

2. Don't post too much personal information: Don't post your location, full name, address, phone number or email address. That makes it too easy to create a fake profile of your information. It also makes it easy for someone to attempt to secure credit in your name, and create other social media accounts in your name.

3. Google your name and/or nickname for any fake profiles that might exist about you or your child: Should you find such a profile, contact the owner of the app or website. If you're a teen, tell a parent, teacher, or school resource officer.

4. Make your passwords strong and Don't Share: Use strong passwords and change them often. Don't share the password with friends.

5. As we said earlier, be careful when using free Wi-Fi or a public computer: First and foremost, you should always sign out of your accounts when finished. If you're using a public computer and don't sign out, others can access your password and information. Also, when using Wi-Fi, it might be easy to record your keystrokes or even access your account if a user on that same network is using the right software.

Too Late! It Happened to My Child. What Can I Do Now?

I recommend the following steps for anyone that has had their information hijacked:

1. **Record the evidence:** This includes screen grabs. Or print any posts that have been directed at or about you.

2. **Talk to your teacher, coach, school counselor or principal:** As I mentioned earlier, most schools in the US and in other western countries have "responsible use of technology" policies that cover cyber bullying and identity theft. If the person involved in such activity attends the same school as the victim, the school may provide more options than the legal authorities. However, ultimately, you'll want to contact the police if the issue can't be resolved through the school. See my next point.

3. **Report it to the police:** If you believe you are the victim of one of the crimes explained above, you should report it to the police. However, if your situation involves a nude or sexual image of a young person, you might want to consider obtaining legal advice before going to the police. Each state varies as to the proper process.

4. **If You Know the Person That Created the Fake Account, Ask them to delete it:** If an account has been created for you, chances are you know who

created the account. If they don't represent a physical threat to you, ask them to delete it. If they refuse to delete it, you should contact a trusted adult, parent, teacher or school resource officer.

5. **Apply for a protection order:** Every so often these issues might involve a potentially dangerous person. If this is the case, and you're being stalked, intimidated or threatened consider applying for a court protection order. In some states, this might be known as a restraining order.

6. **Report the abuse to the app or website owner:** It's important that any fake profile created in your name (or act of cyber bullying) be reported to the app or website owner. For example: If a page has been created in your name, both Facebook, Instagram and many others have a process that you should follow.

Everything Else Has Failed. Are There Other Options?

If you've received no relief from law enforcement or your school, there are steps that you can take to possibly find the individual that created a fake social media account in your name. To do so, you may wish to consider subscribing to a service such as Spokeo.com.

Every new social media account requires an email address at the point of registration. They also require that you provide a different email address in the event they need to contact you. Since email services such as Gmail and Yahoo are so easy to create, often offenders quickly create a new email account using one of these two services. These email addresses are generally linked to an email account that they actually use.

If you know the email address that is associated with the fake social media account that is in your name, Spokeo can often find other emails created by the person who used that address to create that account.

For example: If a student named John Doe created a fake Instagram account related to James Johnson, he would have likely used another email account to do so. To that end, if he created an email account named jamesjohnson#1977@gmail.com — Google makes him use an existing email account that can be used in the event Google needs to contact him.

Spokeo searches all email names that have been used to create such accounts. If John Doe does not have his privacy settings set to friends only — there is a good chance his real email and name will be displayed during the Spokeo search.

Lastly, if you think you know who created the fake social media account, and you have a name, phone number or email address for the person, Spokeo will also find most email addresses and social media accounts created by that person. If your fake page was created by the individual under suspicion, there is a chance it will appear during your Spokeo search.

Unfortunately, no approach is guaranteed to work every time. However, if it does, James Johnson now has the person's name that created the fake account – and perhaps many others. At that point, James' parents can contact John Doe's parents, school or the police.

THE WILD-WILD WEST

We are very much living in the era of the wild-wild-west when it comes to policing digital ne'er-do-wells.

Technology that was created to help bring society together often is used to break it apart. In schools, the petty jealousies, and popular cliques of the past continue today – but are emboldened due to the scope, power and at times the perception that social media is anonymous.

The greatest means of protecting your family's online communication is to keep the lines of communication open at home. Children know what is going on at their school and with their friends. They often know when other children are having problems with classmates in the school or online. Knowledge and subsequent action is key to circumventing problems.

Make certain your children understand some of the points we've addressed in this chapter. However, understand that with the constant evolution of apps, it takes vigilance to keep ahead of those that might not have your best interest at heart.

As the wise elderly nun taught me, you're never too old to learn.

THE BIG GREEN BRAIN

In 1899, while Samuel Clemens, aka, Mark Twain was living in Sweden, he wrote an article that was eventually published in *Harper's Monthly Magazine* about fifteen years later. In his essay, Clemens waxed poetically about the use of pictures as memory devices. Given his many tours on the speaker's circuit, Clemens often used images in place of notes when he delivered his speeches.

Clemens said, *"...you can tear up your pictures as soon as you have made them—they will stay fresh and strong in your memory in the order and sequence in which you scratched them down."* Given his success with this method, he felt these "tricks" would help children absorb the lessons of history.

I spend many hours each week, heeding his advice attempting to find just the right image or video to help students better understand the good, the bad and the ugly consequences of social media. A few years ago, I was looking for such images when I came upon an animated video of a transparent head with a green brain floating and slowly rotating through the ethers of the universe. I was captivated by its outwardly omnipresent form — which seemed to possess the ability to see, know and tell all — while having no empathy for its victims.

I needed that big green brain to tell the story. The story of how digital devices and the corresponding apps potentially see everything that you do; record everything that you do; and potentially distribute everything that you do. So, with the help of $25, I purchased the digital rights to the big green brain and set out to tell the story.

Perhaps no better example of the big green brain's power was exhibited by Curt Schilling, the former baseball great that put the hurt on two "virtual thugs" who hid behind pseudonyms as they trash talked Curt Schilling's daughter with rude, misogynistic rants on Twitter.

The trash-talking Twitter tantrums were in response to Schillings proud post congratulating his daughter Gabby's acceptance to college where she'll be playing softball. The post was met with a flurry of mean-spirited, highly sexualized and somewhat violent comments directed at Gabby.

Like any self-respecting father, Mr. Schilling's protective shield was raised as he vowed to "out" the craven provocateurs, lashing back and revealing their real names, jobs, and colleges they were attending. I'm sure each was shocked by how quick, accurate and overwhelming Mr. Schillings reply was.

One of the miscreants known on _Twitter_ as "The Sports Guru" was a DJ at Brookdale Community College in New Jersey. He has since been suspended by the school for violating its standard of conduct.

Another virtual assailant purportedly was the VP of the Theta Xi fraternity at Montclair State University and a ticket-seller for the Yankees. Upon learning the identity of the individual, he was subsequently fired by the Yankees. These situations are great illustrations of the power of the big green brain.

DID HE CREATE BIGGER ISSUES FOR HIS FAMILY?

While most fathers, my self-included would stop at nothing to protect our children, I'm not certain that Mr. Schilling didn't create more problems given his response. He now has raised the ire of every self-loathing cretin on the Internet by his "shock and awe" offensive. This only garnered more hate filled responses on social media that followed him and his family.

Additionally, given his public profile, telling the world where his daughter will be attending college is also an invitation for problems. If the "creepy guy down the street" didn't know about Mr. Schilling's daughter — he does now.

TAKE 10

If social media were not a major part of my career, I

might have reacted in much the same way as Mr. Schilling. However, the last slide in our live presentations to teens perhaps provides the best advice for everyone young and old when considering a social media comment... "Take 10."

Before ever sending a tweet, posting a Snap or responding to another user, take 10 seconds, 10 minutes or 10 hours and think about the consequences of your actions. I'm sure The Sports Guru; the VP of the Theta Xi fraternity at Montclair State University; and even Curt Schilling wish they had taken that same advice before they entered 140 characters to elicit laughter or seek revenge.

LOST CAREERS & SOCIAL MEDIA

In the 2016 article in People Magazine, <u>20 Tales of Employees Who Were Fired Because of Social Media Posts</u>, courtesy of <u>Reddit</u>, writer Lydia Price mentioned several cases where employees lost jobs due to inadvisable social media posts. courtesy of Reddit

Of the 20 listed, these three were my favorites:

5. *"A prospective employee at the company I work for had just passed his interview and was told that all he needs to do is pass a drug test and a physical and he would start on Monday. Someone found the new hire on Facebook and the guy had just posted 20 minutes after the interview, 'S—! Anyone know how to pass a drug test in 24 hours?!'"*

6. *"I had to fire an employee for a tweet he wrote about a customer. He tweeted '(customer's full name) would be*

a great name for a porn star.' I found out about it when the customer's lawyer called me the next day threatening action. Turns out the guy worked for the local newspaper and obsessively searched his name on all social media."

13. "A girl I know was a nurse at a hospital and got fired for posting things on Facebook such as: 'Soooooo sleepy here in the ICU. Will someone please code and give me something exciting to do? #isthatbad?' and a lot of racist things. The dumbest part about it was she was TAGGING the hospital she worked at in her posts."

PRIVACY: DIVORCE AND SOCIAL MEDIA

Recently, a study published in the Journal of Cyberpsychology, Behavior and Social Networking, determined that Facebook users that login more than once an hour daily are more prone to "experience Facebook–related conflict" with their better half. Such conflicts often lead to a breakups or divorce. The scientific study was conducted by Russell Clayton, at the University Of Missouri School Of Journalism – in conjunction with a team at the University of Hawaii at Hilo and St. Mary's University in San Antonio. Collectively they surveyed 205 Facebook users between the ages of 18 to 82. 79 percent of these users suggested that they were in the midst of a romantic relationship.

The study's hypothesis was that one's social media use -- particularly over one hour per day --and monitoring of one's partner could lead to relationship issues. The study suggests a correlation between the use of Facebook and the steadiness of the romantic relationship. One might further assume that the same is true for all social media.

You don't need to be a psychologist to understand that

the more time spent focused glaring at a glowing screen is time spent away from a conversation with your partner. Moreover, as other studies have shown, many folks have reconnected with former romantic interested via social media. This was much more difficult prior to the rise of social media.

In a 2015 article in the Huffington Post, titled, New Survey Says, Stay Off Social Media (Or Risk Divorce), Brittany Wong wrote:

"...Divorce attorneys agree that social media has increasingly played a part in marriage breakdowns. In 2010, 81 percent of divorce attorneys surveyed by the American Academy of Matrimonial Lawyers said they'd seen an increase in the number of cases using social networking evidence in the five years prior. The attorneys said Facebook was the number one source for finding online evidence, with 66 percent admitting they'd found evidence by combing the site."

It probably didn't take a survey to determine these results. However, it helps to prove the point. There is limited time per day. The more time you spend on social media is the time you can't spend with your partner or child.

DATA, DATA, DATA

Today, data from government, marketing companies, and social media are easily aggregated and bought and sold. It's often easy to determine the real names of so called "alias Cowboys" by simply knowing just one identifying piece of information, such as their pseudonym, email address, home address or other information. As I mentioned earlier, services such as US

SEARCH, Intelius, and others aggregate databases from auditor's sites, court records, social media sites and other publications often with incredible accuracy. The cloak of darkness for most such offenders is often quickly eliminated — particularly by people with the financial means such as Schilling. However, most of these services cost less than $10.00 per month and often will surprise you by the richness of information it has on almost everyone.

Privacy does not exist.

Chapter 5 – Pornography

As you've probably guessed by now, I'm quite fond of reminiscing on more simple times. Although from a distance the grass always looks greener. However, life was in some ways likely a challenge for our parents as well during the era of black and white.

That said, I can't imagine what it was like raising kids in the 1960's. There are many TV shows that paint a somewhat idyllic portrait of life during those times. LEAVE IT TO BEAVER, was one of my favorite programs. I recall one episode that depicted the rather simple problems that Larry Mondello's parents had raising that chubby, not very bright classmate of the "Beave."

SCRIPT EXCERPT

Theodore "Beaver" Cleaver: *You wanna' mess around later?*

Larry Mondello: *I can't, I'm grounded.*

Theodore "Beaver" Cleaver: *How come?*

Larry Mondello: *My father caught me eating pie in bed.*

Ah... what parent wouldn't give a week's pay to have such issues today? Yet, the 1960's was the start of an era that launched the famous Jacobellis v. Ohio obscenity case.

But what actually is obscenity? *"I know it when I see it"* was famously written by United States Supreme Court Justice Potter Stewart in 1964 to describe his view of obscenity in that same case.

Stewart wrote:

"I shall not today attempt further to define the kinds of material I understand to be embraced within that shorthand description ["hard-core pornography"], and perhaps I could never succeed in intelligibly doing so. But I know it when I see it, and the motion picture involved in this case is not that."

I wonder if he saw those images in brilliant colors and in 3D if he would have changed his mind. I wonder if he envisioned an era when every kind of pornography would immediately be available to every teen in 2017, 2018 and beyond? The answer: Of course not.

The images in question were tame compared to current standards. Today's TV commercials for Victoria's Secret might often be more revealing – or at least as seductive – to the 13-year-old boy whose evening TV show is interrupted by half-naked models selling... well, you know what they're selling.

It's difficult today for teens to navigate their own insecurities — as their minds are fueled by raging hormones and their eyes and ears flooded by media's ideals of the perfect man or woman.

Sex sells everything from hamburgers – to cars – to beer… and we wonder why children are confused, restless, self-absorbed and often feel painfully inadequate.

Add to the equation the aforementioned 7×24 access to pornography via the web, and it's a recipe for rewired brains and a change in how this generation views intimacy.

THE ORIGINS OF PORNOGRAPHY

Where did this all begin? Frankly, pornography has been around since man first scratched crude illustrations on cave walls. Around 1440, thanks to our good friend German inventor *Johannes Gutenberg,* man discovered that he could print multiple copies of the Bible – or as others would discover -- distribute pornography to the masses.

Then again in 1749, erotic graphic art was widely created and distributed in Paris, eventually coming to be known by many as "French postcards."

Although we think of pornographic films as a recent phenomenon – in the era of the roaring 20's — they were widely available to what we thought was a tame, puritanical society.

ENOUGH IS NOT ENOUGH

Perhaps thanks to the mainstreaming of pornography from the likes of the *"silk-pajamaed"* Hugh Hefner in the 1950's – viewers wanted more than the printed naked pictures in Playboy. Thus by the 1960s pornographic films surged.

The growth continued with the development of

videocassettes in the 1980s — and with DVDs, in the 1990s the pornography industry continued to grow. However, perhaps no one saw what was on the horizon with the Internet.

Beyond simply creating an immense marketplace for pornography — the Internet also encouraged many amateurs to post images of themselves. The use of webcams opened the industry even further — allowing individuals to post their activity LIVE. Sadly, the Internet also increased the availability of child pornography.

By now you might be thinking, "What does this have to do with my child?" The answer: A Lot.

TEEN PORNOGRAPHY CONSUMPTION STATISTICS

What we think of today as "run-of-the-mill" pornography is being consumed by our children in unheard of numbers. With Virtual Reality, it's about to get worse.

According to Therapy Associates, a Utah based professional assessment and treatment service for children, teens, parents, and families –, this is just a small part of what our kids are exposed to today:

- The average age a child first sees internet pornography is 11
- 93 % of boys and 62% of girls are exposed to internet pornography before the age of 18
- 70% of young men ages 18-24 visit pornographic websites on at least a monthly basis
- 35% of boys have done this on at least ten occasions
- 83% of boys have seen group sex on the internet
- 56% of divorce cases involve one party having an

obsessive interest in online porn

- 12% of websites on the internet are pornographic
- 25% of search engine requests each day are pornography related—approximately 70 million per day
- Only 3% of pornographic websites require age verification
- The most popular day of the week for viewing pornography is Sunday.

As teens and tweens become accustomed to porn, the next images need to be even more sensational in order to keep their interest and increase the level of dopamine to satisfy their cravings. This often impacts a user's ability to sustain relationships with their girlfriend and boyfriends, wives and spouses. Each new experience requires an even greater, more daring visual image.

Thus, enters the world of Virtual Reality and the images that it offers. But first let's address the devices before the vices:

THE DEVICES & VICES

There are many developers of new Virtual Reality devices and content. Oculus, Samsung, HTC, Google, and Sony are but a few. However, just to better define the interest as it relates to porn — consider the terms, "virtual reality porn" and "virtual reality sex" are two of the top 10 keywords for searches related to Virtual Reality.

In Japan during the spring of 2016, a virtual reality pornography festival was forced to close due to overcrowding. The venue was too small to accommodate the crowd.

Further, as NEWSWEEK TECH writer, Seung Lee wrote in his June, 16th 2016 article following his first encounter with VR Porn, *"The moment I knew that virtual reality porn worked was when the naked, voluptuous woman began an oil massage as I rested in an armchair in a tropical vacation house in Hawaii. The message escalated to sex in a hurry."*

As parents, we must be aware that a child's brain – in the best of homes – is not completely wired until well after their teen years. However, exposure to pornography can rewire an already underdeveloped brain before its time.

This overstimulation of the reward circuitry through *dopamine spikes* resulting from viewing pornography— creates desensitization. When dopamine receptors drop after too much stimulation, the brain will not respond as it had in the past. As such, there is less reward from the pleasure.

Now, back to our chubby friend Larry Modello in the 1960's. Perhaps eating one Moon Pie satisfied his appetite. But after a while, he'd need two and then three... you get the picture.

This leads users to search even harder for feelings of satisfaction such as for longer porn sessions, with more frequency – and today through the ultimate porn experience – Virtual Reality.

A question for all of us: Once Virtual Reality becomes as popular as Internet porn – what will happen to intimacy between couples? What happens to families? What then happens to society?

YOUTUBE & PORN

The overwhelming majority of teens use YouTube. In fact, in our recent survey of middle and high school students, YouTube was the number one app on their phones. However, type "VIRTUAL REALITY PORN" in the YouTube search bar, and you'll be deluged with search returns with titles such as:

- WIFE CATCHES HER HUSBAND WATCHING VIRTUAL REALITY PORN
- TRYING VIRTUAL REALITY PORN WITH MY DATE
- VIRTUAL REALITY PORN IS HERE, AND IT'S SCARY REALISTIC
- VIRTUAL REALITY PORN WITH NIKKI

If you're not filtering YouTube on your child's device – your child already has access to the images and information related to accessing true, 3D virtual reality. Since less than 50% of parents monitor what their children do on their devices, this has become a significant issue for families.

RESOURCES

Because research suggests that most pornography and sexual addictions begin during adolescence, Therapy Associates based in Utah, provide a very informative paper titled: Navigating Pornography Addiction a Guide for Parents

Additionally, I highly recommend that parents view the documentary produced by Channel 4 in the UK entitled: Channel 4Ponrography and the brain:

As the Channel 4 program illustrates, with teens, the patterns of brain activity when viewing porn, are very similar to those of individuals with drug and alcohol addictions when they view pictures of alcohol and drugs.

It is clear that it can create problems for some adolescents and young adults who use it. Moreover, as mentioned earlier, it's not just the addiction – it's how these young people will view intimacy and relationships as they get older.

So where do you go from here? I suggest you read our last chapter – which will help you better manage your child's online activity and minimize problems for them in the future.

Virtual Pornography, which will likely be available in app stores soon – and can already be integrated with your child's phone and certain VR gaming system headsets – is nothing more than another app. As such, it will be part of every parent's responsibility to manage their child's activity.

Parenting today is many ways is much harder than in the days of LEAVE IT TO BEAVER. The temptations and access to pornography are greater at a time when both parents are working and have less time to parent. Getting your arms around the technology and temptations must start today.

Although technology is responsible for so much good in the lives of our children – I'm sure most of us would love a day when the biggest issue we face is our children eating a moon pie in bed.

Chapter 6 – Mental Health

We have likely all seen this situation before. You go to your favorite fast food restaurant to buy a cup of coffee or burger, and the employee behind the POS Terminal is a young teen boy or girl. They take your order, and while giving you your change, you notice scars on their arms. Were they burned by the deep fryer? No. Most likely they participated in the ugly trend of cutting.

Having been married to a teacher for over 40 years, I was keenly aware of the issue where teens use self-harm as a coping mechanism. Somehow, the cutting of the skin and subsequent bleeding brings a sense of relief to the problems of their lives. Sadly, I see this all too often in my travels to area schools. In fact, speak to any guidance counselor in a middle school, and they can likely tell you story upon story of teens and tweens that have sought such relief.

Anxiety concerning divorce, grades, and relationships,

abuse in the home, financial hardships, sexual identity, bullying and any other problem can bring on such actions. Many children hide these marks from their parents – choosing parts of their body that go unseen by Mom and Dad.

Many in the mental health field believe that self-harm is on the rise, and perhaps is one of the most troubling symptoms of a wider psychological problem that plagues 21st-century adolescents.

Teen depression and anxiety have been escalating since 2012 after several years of stability. It's an occurrence without demographic bounds. As I have seen in my own travels – it cuts across the inner-city, through suburban towns and rural townships. It doesn't care if you're white, black, Asian, Hispanic, gay, transgender, straight, rich or poor.

According to a 2015 study by the Department of Health and Human Services, about 3 million teens between the ages of 12 to 17 have had at least one major depressive episode in the past year. Additionally, at least 2 million reported experiencing depression that hurt their ability to function on a daily basis. Perhaps even more perplexing, according to data from the National Institute of Mental Health, approximately 6.3 million teens--have had an anxiety disorder.

In a May 2017 study in Translational Psychiatry, researchers found that *"Projecting from age-specific incidence proportions, the cumulative incidence of depression between the ages of 12 and 17 is 13.6% among male and 36.1% among female subjects. The sex difference in incidence is significant at the age of 12 years.*

To put teen mental health concerns into even closer perspective, consider these stats from Cincinnati Children's Hospital:

The number of youth mental-health assessments in Cincinnati Children's emergency department rose from 4,362 in the fiscal year 2011 to 7,864 by mid-2017. This equals a 10% increase, year over year. Moreover, as we mentioned in an earlier chapter, Cincinnati Children's Hospital has seen a 70% increase of children treated for anxiety and depression between 2011 and 2015.

Additionally, in the Greater Cincinnati area – which has a population of about 2.2 million people, there were 16 adolescent suicides between January and June of 2017. Certainly, not a record anyone hopes is broken.

SOCIAL MEDIA & TEEN MENTAL HEALTH

Rachel Ehmke, of CHILD MIND INSTITUE, writes in her article HOW USING SOCIAL MEDIA IMPACTS TEENAGERS says, *"Peer acceptance is a big thing for adolescents, and many of them care about their image as much as a politician running for office, and to them, it can feel as serious. Add to that the fact that kids today are getting actual polling data on how much people like them or their appearance via things like "likes." It's enough to turn anyone's head. Who wouldn't want to make herself look cooler if she can? So kids can spend hours pruning their online identities, trying to project an idealized image. Teenage girls sort through hundreds of photos, agonizing over which ones to post online. Boys compete for attention by trying to out-gross one other, pushing the envelope as much as they can in the already disinhibited atmosphere online. Kids gang up on each other."*

I'll often say to groups of approximately 100 students, *"Understand that almost 25 of your classmates are going through a difficult time right now. How you treat them to their face – and online can lift them up – or push them into a deeper hole."*

In our 2016 survey of nearly 10,000 students between the ages of 12 and 19 about 18% of respondents said they had been bullied online. Over 20% stated they have suffered through depression. Many of the students felt that such online negativity toward each other lead to their depression.

Some of their unedited comments shed light on teen's online life:

- They text a lot and also sometimes will spread rumors about people. Also at one time, there was an Instagram account called DMS crushes that could spread rumors or private information.

- People are making accounts about students and not revealing who they are.

- People are constantly on social media, always posting. Also, people who post rude things about other people.

- I've heard that a person took a vid of their sister naked and showed it to someone

- The new trend is creating "spam" accounts where teenagers make their profile private and only let certain friends follow them. They post funny, rude, and personal things that they wouldn't like the rest of the school/world to see. What they don't know is that their profiles are not as private as they think.

- Here's what sucks. It's that no matter what you do, people will still find a way around it. People still won't care and disregard everything said to them. This generation is disgusting. Everybody is offended by everything and other people just trying to live normal lives are affected by them, and they're over protective parents who couldn't dare to imagine their kid's stupid third world gender that doesn't even exist. No matter what anybody does, this problem will not be fixed. Ever. It's been around since the beginning of time. So until people learn to stand up for themselves, and take control of themselves, nothing will get better. Social media is just the feeling place, and quite frankly, just the beginning of something great and horrible.

- People become fake when they get on social media as they change their personality to fit society's image of how they should be.

- People send mass nudes images. I could receive like 20 in one day if I wanted

- They are very rude and don't consider people's feelings at all.

- Some people use it to blackmail people with pictures.

- Unfortunately, yes, even at my age nudes are sent. But it's really hard to be shielded from everything inappropriate online, so just trust that most of us will be responsible.

- No, I don't bully people online I get bullied online

- Some kids post embarrassing photos of other people or even their friends that hurt their feelings.

- People get into fights 24/7 on Social Media Sites

In some respects, these are the same petty issues as years past. However, there are trends today that take place both in and out of school hours – 24 hours per day. This constant barrage of "teen commentary and comparison" makes teen life more difficult – particularly when you consider they often have no physical or time boundaries.

As we have found in our own discussions with school counselors – depression and anxiety are often under reported by the teens themselves. Although most children would willingly report a broken leg, fever or stomach issues, there continues to be a stigma attached to mental health issues. Therefore, health care professionals often can't help until the problem becomes obvious. At that point, it could be too late.

In fact, according to a 2015 report from the Child Mind

Institute, it was determined that only about 20% of young people with a diagnosable anxiety disorder get treatment.

In her October 27th, 2016 article in **TIME MAGAZINE, Teen Depression, and Anxiety: Why the Kids Are Not Alright** writer Susanna Schrobsdorff said:

In my dozens of conversations with teens, parents, clinicians and school counselors across the country, there was a pervasive sense that being a teenager today is a draining full-time job that includes doing schoolwork, managing a social-media identity and fretting about career, climate change, sexism, racism--you name it. Every fight or slight is documented online for hours or days after the incident. It's exhausting.

And yet we have given digital devices to our kids and in many cases exasperated the problems. We've not provided or demanded technology free zones. Kids have unfettered access to everyone 7 days per week, 365 days per year. Conversely, the world has access to them as well.

Teens are often comparing their lives, their bodies, their accomplishments to those of their peers or even the celebrities that they admire.

Additionally, as parents, we are often physically present but mentally absent from their lives – as we glare at the glowing screen in our own hands -- comparing our family, our home, our boat, our car, our kids, our spouses to the many friends and acquaintances in our "friends" list. Although we wonder if our kids listen to us – I can tell you that they do observe us.

Empathy & Narcissism

Narcissism is a growing concern among mental health care provider throughout our country. Social media and poor parenting are sometimes defined as the main culprits in building teenagers that are self-centered and insecure. However, by nature, teens are self-centered and insecure. Most children are still trying to understand life – create real assessments about themselves – while developing judgment skills. They also still feel that they are impervious to life's consequences.

In reality, there is generally never one reason for the growth of any one disease, societal ill or cultural trend. However, there is no denying that there is a growing lack of empathy among teens and their peers.

Patricia J. Manney, an American writer, and speaker posted an Op Ed in the June 2015 edition of Live Science. In her post titled, <u>Is Technology Destroying Empathy?</u> she wrote:

I had explored empathy creation since 2008 when I published a paper entitled "Empathy in the Time of Technology: How Storytelling is the Key to Empathy" in the Journal of Evolution and Technology. Empathy works on a neurological system that scientists are still trying to understand, involving a "theory of mind network" that includes emulation and learning. But at the center of empathy creation is communication.

…. But for all that information and exposure to new ideas, there are many examples of communication technologies that can destroy empathy. Let's begin with the ideological information silos of broadcast, print,

website and social media, where conservatives or liberals only listen, read and watch their own thoughts repeated in recursive echo chambers of increasingly radical and exclusionary thought.

Having visited with nearly 400 schools over the past 5 years, I have seen how teens and adults tend to get their information from a few select sources. They often share concepts and articles from these sources and consequently have a limited view of the world and each other. There are seldom opposing views allowed. And when such views are voiced they are sometimes shouted down, or the opposing individual is bullied.

We, of course, see this in adult life via cable TV news. For example, each news network, admittedly or not, has its own perspective on what is news. If we only follow one news source – which often happens – we have a limited view of the world. Our patience and knowledge for opposing views become limited. We grow angry and assume the worse of many from the other side. We lose our empathy.

This trend had created division within our country. It ultimately demonizes or dehumanizes the opposing point of view. It's very easy to see when observing political debate. It's everywhere, 7 days a week, 24 hours per day.

Now take this theory and apply it to teen life.

Imagine what you see on TV where democrats and republicans scrutinize every word, turn of a phrase, choice of tie our haircut and then transition that concept to your child's social group.

Particularly for girls, their completion, body type,

make-up, jewelry, shoes, and clothes are under constant scrutiny. They repetitively track their likes on Instagram as if it validates them as humans. Not enough likes? Take down the post and do a better job of curating your photos in the future.

As adults, we understand what I call "spin media." Not everything we see and hear is true. Children can't often discern what they see and hear – and sometimes don't hear -- within their peer group.

If a child is facing other stressors in their life – and they feel their peer group is defaming them or ignoring them – it can be the proverbial straw that "breaks the camel's back."

As we know, children grow physically in their early teen years. But what is unseen is the mental growth that takes place. For example, Face-to-face interaction is vital to learning how to read and express emotion. However, 60% of the synapses in the brain disappears if they aren't used between birth and adolescence. Since the national daily average for teens being online is nearly seven hours a day, one might assume that their emotional IQ will be negatively impacted.

Not all is bad. There is evidence that social media can offer our children positive emotional benefits. For example, Teens can and do often connect with their peers more easily through social media and texting and messaging apps. As such, they often feel supported through their network of *positive,* online friends. The key word is "positive" online friends.

With these networks and online stories, they can be exposed to information and other's life experiences that they might not have otherwise witnessed. This can be very positive – or at times negative.

DEPRESSION & SUICIDE

In a recent study by the International Center for Media & the Public Affairs (ICMPA) study, *"students around the world reported that being tethered to digital technology 24/7 is not just a habit, it is essential to the way they construct and manage their friendships and social lives."*

It's easy to read news accounts of social media "gone bad" and determine that no child should have access to this "heathen devil' technology. Social media and technology are often used for more good purposes than bad. Yet we can't overlook the inherent dangers that exist when it is misused.

Sadly, part of my job takes me to places I'd rather not be. I'd rather not hear the painful social media stories that children often share with me. I'd rather not hear the stories that parents share concerning their child's addiction to online pornography.

I'd rather not hear stories concerning a child being hospitalized due to suicide ideation – or a child being buried due to death by suicide.

I'd rather not hear about a 13-year old's depression due to a naked photo she sent to her boyfriend being shared at the school.

Yet this is why this book is written -- to cast light on a subject that is so often swept under the carpet of our society.

It amazes me that with new studies showing how the increased use of apps such as Facebook and Instagram is correlated with low self-esteem and decreased life satisfaction. We now know that the constant over stimulation created by social networking can turn the nervous system into fight-or-flight mode, which makes teen depression and anxiety worse.

This problem is amplified when we consider that seventy-six percent of teens use social media, and 50 percent of teens feel they are addicted to their mobile devices.

By June 2017 in Greater Cincinnati, 15 teens and an 8-year-old took their own lives. It was an unprecedented number in this beautiful river city. This trend is exhibited throughout the US. In fact, one of the wealthiest areas in the United States has one of the highest teen suicide rates in the country.

According to a 2017 CDC Report in the March 3rd Mercury News, during the period 2003 to 2015, Palo Alto's youth suicide rate per 100,000 people was 14.1. The national average is 5.4.

Epidemiologic Assistance (Epi-Aid) studies which are performed by the CDC address urgent public health problems ranging from outbreaks of infectious diseases; effects of natural disasters and deaths by suicide.

According to the CDC, such reports that focus on death by suicide include:

- Capturing trends in fatal and nonfatal suicidal behaviors in youths, including the number of deaths, visits to emergency rooms and hospital discharges
- Examination of whether print media coverage of suicides meet guidelines suggested by mental

health professionals

- Inventory and comparison of local youth suicide prevention programs; policies related to national recommendations; and making recommendations on strategies for the school, community and county levels.

In the Palo Alto case, researchers reviewed 246 articles that addressed suicide deaths and determined that media outlets did not follow proper suicide reporting guidelines. Such guidelines caution against sharing too much detail related to the method of suicide, photographs of memorials or grieving relatives and friends. This is all part of what is called the contagion theory.

There is a theory that too much focus on suicide and even the romanticizing of death by suicide can create a contagious response by others. In fact, in the case of the death of suicide of Jessica Logan, she had just attended a friend's funeral who died at his own hands. She returned home and took her own life.

THE ISSUE OF LIVE STREAMING SUICIDES

In her July 6, 2017, article in Philly.com, titled, **Livestream suicides: Does it influence our kids,** Terri Erbacher, Ph.D., Clinical Associate Professor, Philadelphia College of Osteopathic Medicine wrote:

"Now, with the advent of Facebook Live, social media is another avenue for our youth to unexpectedly view violence. Since it began in 2015, more than more than 45 acts of violence--including suicide—have been live streamed for the world to see.

Livestream suicides greatly increase the number of persons exposed, which increases the possibility of contagion—*the phenomenon through which exposure to suicide can lead to another's suicide attempt. This is particularly troublesome among adolescents who may already be struggling, and perhaps contemplating suicide."*

The contagion effect has been studied since the 1990's by the Center for Decease Control. In their paper, the CDC reported:

"One risk factor that has emerged from this research is suicide "contagion," a process by which exposure to the suicide or suicidal behavior of one or more persons influences others to commit or attempt suicide. Evidence suggests that the effect of contagion is not confined to suicides occurring in discrete geographic areas. In particular, nonfictional newspaper and television coverage of suicide has been associated with a statistically significant excess of suicides. The effect of contagion appears to be strongest among adolescents, and several well publicized "clusters" among young persons have occurred.

These findings have induced efforts on the part of many suicide- prevention specialists, public health practitioners, and researchers to curtail the reporting of suicide -- especially youth suicide -- in newspapers and on television. Such efforts were often counterproductive, and news articles about suicides were written without the valuable input of well- informed suicide-prevention specialists and others in the community."

Today, news media generally does a better job of being sensitive to how they report suicides. Yet, at times we still see news programs depicting mourning families and friends, impromptu memorials, and interviews with those that knew the victim. Although we can't hide reality from our kids, we, as a society, need to make certain we are not sensationalizing or glorifying such acts. To a child struggling with their own internal issues, it can create additional trauma.

THIRTEEN REASONS WHY

Then there is the concern over the original Netflix TV series, Thirteen Reasons Why. According to the Netflix program information:

"Katherine Langford plays the role of Hannah, a young woman who takes her own life. Two weeks after her tragic death, a classmate named Clay finds a mysterious box on his porch. Inside the box are recordings made by Hannah -- on whom Clay had a crush -- in which she explains the 13 reasons why she chose to commit suicide. If Clay decides to listen to the recordings, he will find out if and how he made a list. This intricate and heart-wrenching tale is told through Clay and Hannah's dual narratives."

Although the program is well done and sheds a bright light on an issue that is plaguing our nation, there is concern among mental health care providers that the program might only add to the problem.

Recently, there had been a series of teens take their lives using live broadcast apps. Shobhit Negi, a Psychiatrist in Howard County, Maryland, shed some light on the issue in the Baltimore Sun article Teens Turn to Social Media for Attention, Even in Death.

"Posting to the world the deliberate act of ending one's life can possibly serve different purposes. The combination of the quasi-feeling of connectedness

instilled by social media and the feeling that one can control one's actions in the privacy of the bedroom or bathroom might take away the solitary feeling of the suicide act. The combined weight of vulnerability, need for validation and limited decision-making capacity might make it difficult for some youth to step back once they have posted something pertaining to suicide on social media."

To my knowledge, in the past 5 years, I have known only a few students who went on to take their lives. However, I have heard many stories from teens about how they or their relatives have been hospitalized – or in some cases taken their life.

The first situation involved a 12-year-old girl whose mom approached me at a presentation. Her daughter, who I'll call Monica, had become a victim of identity theft when another student created a fake Instagram page in her name and then populated the page with pornography of a girl performing sex acts.

Monica, her mom, and Monica's best friend asked me to help find the person who posted the images and the fake account. I referred them to the police chief that was standing no more than 10 feet from me. However, I gave the mother my card and asked her to contact me if the police chief couldn't help.

About two weeks later I got a call from the mother. She wanted to tell me that Monica had suffered significantly over the past two weeks. The embarrassment and humiliation were difficult for a 12-year-old mind to manage. She then went on to tell me that they found the person responsible for the posting. To my surprise, the offender was Monica's best friend.

Apparently, Monica was receiving attention from boys at the school. Monica's friend was jealous of the attention and decided the humiliate Monica.

In another case, a young man approached me following a presentation to a group of high school students at small, Catholic high school. The boy thanked me for the presentation and then told me, "You're right." I asked him what he meant by his comment. He went on to tell me that his cousin had taken his own life when someone created a fake Instagram page and populate it with homosexual pornography. He told me that the police attempted to track down the offender but had no luck.

Knowing the digital footprint that such actions almost always leave behind, I contacted the local prosecutor about the case. However, when we dug a little deeper, we discovered that indeed the culprit had been found – in Europe.

How the young man that had taken his life was humiliated by someone in Europe is still unknown. Yet, as I point out in my presentations, it's difficult to escape the metadata – or digital tattoo that is left behind during any online communication.

There are countless other stories I could share about my experiences. Most of them today tend to blend in with one another. So many times, the stories are the same. Only the student and school generally differ. However, almost always there is an element of anxiety and depression that either result from the experience – or the experience is due to the depression, anxiety or lack of self-esteem.

So what can parents do?

First, we must watch the warning signs and determine quickly and consider getting our child a professional assessment and treatment if necessary. Again, remember, teen depression and anxiety have been on the rise for over 10 years. There has been much research that suggests that teens displaying symptoms of depression and/or anxiety are not getting the proper treatment.

As we will detail in our last chapter, the parent must place parameters on a child's online time, their access to certain apps and the places where they may use technology. Bedrooms and bathrooms should be off-limits. This is where many intimate conversations take place. Often these conversations lead to actions that will further a child's stress.

We as parents must continue to speak with our kids – not to them. Understand why your child wants to use technology and certain apps. Communication with your child is the key to good parenting.

Also, be certain that your child subscribes to the rule of good living: Body, Mind, and Spirit. Life is about balance and is the pillar of success. How they sleep, what they eat, and their outdoor activity is just as important as the grades they get in school.

We will go into greater detail about managing and monitoring your child's online activity in our final chapter.

ONLINE GAMING & GRIEFING

For the past 20 years, I have taught Catholic CCD and PSR classes at my parish to 6th graders each Tuesday evening. My first year of teaching was 1997. That year, the video game business was growing with such platforms and Nintendo 64 and PS1.

For those of you of a certain age, you might recall the release of the Palm Pilot that year as well. Every self-respecting business person in the IT industry was ditching their Franklin Calendars for a Palm or other PDA device.

A few years later, in April of 2000, the first Blackberry Smartphone made its way to the market – usurping the Palm Pilots, Trios and HandSpring devices of that era.

However, for the kids in my class, they seemed to be unaffected by the change in technology. Few of their parents had Blackberry Smartphones or PDAs.

However, I noticed a shift by 2010 as more families purchased iPhones and later iPods, DSi's and other Wi-Fi enabled platforms. It was at this time the first student approached me about being bullied online by a 35-year-old man.

Wi-Fi has brought incredible benefits to our world. However, it also has brought to your child's door pedophiles and bullies under the auspices of competitive game play. These actions are often called "griefing" or "trolling."

Gamepedia.com defines griefing as:

"Griefing is the act of irritating and angering people in video games through the use of destruction, construction, or social engineering. Popularized in Minecraft by teams, griefing has become a serious problem for server administrators who wish to foster building and protect builders. Most players tend to dislike and frown upon griefing, while others feel it adds a certain degree of drama to the game. Trolling, while most thought very similar to grieving, is not always known as the same thing.

Griefing is normally malicious, while "trolling" is usually used in more of a joking manner."

Whether one's actions are meant to destroy, anger or to joke, such activity can play havoc with a teen who is already under stress in other areas of their lives.

In his March 2017 article, <u>Bullying's newest frontier: Rise of gaming's online abuse and 'griefing,'</u> Alastair <u>Roberts</u> defined griefing in even more detail.

"Online abuse in gaming or 'griefing' has become a popular form of entertainment for some gamers. If you search 'griefing' in YouTube you will come across thousands of videos that advertise themselves with "...made them cry" or "...kid cries," these videos often involve adults or teens purposefully targeting young users within the game and intentionally acting in a way to anger or upset the player. "

Certainly, the anonymous nature of online gaming and internet communication makes many of us bolder. However, the growing lack of empathy that we mentioned earlier, likely plays another role in this trend.

PEDOPHILES & GAMING

The issue of pedophiles is another great concern for parents whose children are using such online games.

In April of 2017, a mother of an 8-year-old boy told the <u>NBC affiliate in New York City</u> that her son was "groomed" by a sexual predator on the popular Roblox game. Roblox has over 50 million monthly users and allows each player to chat with other users. Sadly, this is how the boy was apparently targeted.

According to the mother, the predator portrayed himself as another child – and would often partner with him while playing the game against others. However, the discussions escalated to personal questions and request for photographs.

Google "pedophiles and video gaming," and you'll read countless similar stories – many ending more ruthlessly than in this example.

HELP FOR MENTAL HEALTH ISSUES

Each time that I present to teens I walk that tight-rope of defining real world consequences for kids that misuse technology. I try to make certain kids know that their lives are not over if they experience digital persecution from peers – or if they make a mistake online. Life can go on.

As parents, teachers, clergy, and mentors we must understand that we are blessed to have many resources to help teens and their families deal with this brave new world. Beyond A Wired Family, there are many websites, apps and books to help. One resource to help better understand cyber bullying is the Cyberbullying Research Center. This site can help you better understand social media's place in self-esteem development.

If you feel your child is being harassed online, intervention programs can certainly help both you and your child. Consider visiting the National Suicide Prevention Lifeline or the Substance Abuse and Mental Health Services Administration's (SAMHSA) What a Difference a Friend Makes website.

Remember, social media is NOT the only cause of depression, anxiety, and suicide ideation. However, we would be naïve to think that the growth of such issues is not somehow a significant contributing factor. By understanding the trends of technology and how your child uses social media, you stand a better chance of protecting your child from the temptations and dangers of this evolving world.

We'll discuss how in our next chapter.

Chapter 7 – Managing Your Child's Online Activity

Remember the playground game <u>Simon Says</u>? Back in the day, I use to think of myself as the Steph Curry or LeBron James of that game — capable of isolating the world around me — laser focused on instructions; ready to defeat my weaker, less skilled opponent. That was before the time school playgrounds were filled with hundreds of students with heads tilted forward, squinting to see the latest Snap Chat image or Internet Meme.

Like most popular games, Simon Says went digital in the mid-1980's – several years following the introduction of the greatest accomplishment of mankind at the time, i.e., <u>Pong.</u> During that nascent era, we purchased a Simon Says electronic game for our two daughters. As our oldest child attempted to open the cardboard box that held the device — attached with hard plastic ties that could have foiled Houdini — I anxiously waited to prove my gaming *superiority over every adult, teen, and child within earshot.*

Like every adult male in the room, electronics represented the great "unifier" among men. Whether you were a milquetoast CPA with a penchant for philosophy and culture — or a grizzled dock worker with a stubby cigar perched stubbornly in your teeth– electronic games leveled the playing field, requiring little strength or physical dexterity — and consequently were adopted by all classes and races of people.

However, what I recall most about that game was how good our young daughters were as the complexity of the game increased — and how poor I was as each level of memorization became faster and more intricate. Some things don't get better with age.

Recently, while speaking with a group of parents about the responsible use of technology, I sensed the audience felt much as I did the first time playing the electronic version of Simon Says. The tidal wave of change that has occurred in the communication business — coupled with the incredible proliferation of smart phones and tablets among children has made it difficult for parents to manage their child's online persona and behavior.

But understand, this is important... and your child likely wants your help. As McAfee recently reported, 49% of teens would change their online behavior if they knew that mom or dad was monitoring their activity. Reality suggests most parents don't know where to start.

So where do you begin? As the saying goes, "The journey of a thousand miles starts with the first step."

There is a multitude of strategies you can take to help

manage and monitor your child's online activity. However, the following ten steps are based on conversations I have had with students, teachers, parents, police officers and prosecutors over the past four years. I think you'll find each helpful – but understand, teens are great at circumventing even the best of plans.

TAKE 10 STEPS FORWARD
1. Talk To Your Child & Your Peers
2. Establish A Tech Free Zone In Your Home
3. Own Your Child's iTunes & Google Play Password
4. Check your wireless provider's Account Activity
5. Subscribe to your carrier's Parental Controls
6. Access Other Parental Controls & Your Wireless Router
7. Automatically Backup Your Child's Photos To The Cloud
8. Understand & Audit Your Family's Private Information
9. Keep On Top Of Trends
10. Talk To Your Child Again and Again

Let's take a quick look at each.
1) **Talk to your child and Your Peers**
When working with your child, it's important to set expectations related to appropriate and inappropriate uses of technology. Understand that if your child is at least twelve years old, there is a great likelihood that their

friend's parents have already provided technology to their children. Moreover, your child's friends are already using Instagram, Snap Chat, and Musical.ly. If you choose to allow, your child to have access to such technology you'll need to control what apps are allowed on their devices.

It's also important to speak with your peers; other parents and teachers and share your own experiences. Living in an information age without the benefit of conversation — viewing life only through your own experiences is a bit short-sighted. I have learned more from speaking with teachers, guidance counselors, police officers, students and other parents than I have by simply reading and doing research.

Reach out and start the conversation at your child's school, your neighborhood, and church or recreation center. Share what you know – and listen to what others say.

2) **Create a Tech Free Zone.**

Depending on your child's age, consider creating a tech free zone. This might include the dinner table; bathroom and bedroom. Keep in mind that although technology has increased our ability to communicate with people outside of the home, it has sorely damaged our ability to communicate with those that are most dear to us. In fact, it's reported that one out of five divorces is blamed on Facebook. (Some say as much as 50.%).

The study, which will be published in a forthcoming issue of the Journal of Cyberpsychology, Behavior and Social Networking, found that people who use Facebook excessively are more likely to   succumb to marital or relationship issues.

In fact, an entire website is now devoted to helping people whose relationships have ended due to social media.

Limiting where devices may be used will help reduce the temptation for your child to send something they'll later regret. It might also make you think about limiting your own access to technology.

As for your kids, remember they are children whose brains are not fully wired. As such, their decision-making is severely hampered by hormones; incomplete brain development and lack of experience. They need your help to avoid temptation and misuse of technology. They might hate you today – but they'll thank you tomorrow.

3) Know Their Account Passwords

If your child is under the age of 16, you and only you should create and know the password to your child's iTunes or Google Play account. As a parent, you should be the only person authorized to download apps to that device. Moreover, often, once an app is downloaded there might be another 15 minutes that would allow your child to download other apps without your knowledge. To that end, don't give the device back to your child until you're certain it will require your password for any additional app downloads.

This is important since many apps are available that hide other apps from parents. Often these "stealthy" apps are used to hide photos, text messages, and videos from parents and other adults. Once it's on their device, it might be difficult to find. If you haven't been following this approach, you should go back over your purchase history on iTunes and GooglePlay to see what apps might have been purchased. However, this purchase history might not include those apps that were downloaded for free.

You should also know the passwords to their device – and every app on that device.

4) Check your wireless provider's Account Activity

Although this approach might show your child's call detail and provide a list of numbers that might have been texted by or to your child — the reality is most kids don't use their phone to call people. Moreover, most don't use the texting service provided by their carrier. While this might have been true in 2012, that was a million years ago. Most teens today use Snap Chat, Kik, or Whatsapp for texting. These apps use Wi-Fi or the data plan of the carrier rather than the texting plan. Unfortunately, it is very difficult for parents to "see" these text messages or to even know with whom their child is communicating. Therefore, it is incumbent on you as the parent or guardian to decide what texting app they may use.

Your wireless carrier will provide information on the amount of data being consumed by your child's device — if indeed they are using the carrier's broadband. However, as I mentioned earlier, teens often use the Wi-Fi in the home or where free Wi-Fi is available. If you check your carrier's account activity, you'll at least be armed with some information relative to data consumption and a percentage of texting activity and call detail.

5) Subscribe To Your Carrier's Parental Controls

Although parental controls offered by your carrier won't keep track of each app your child is using, it will allow you to control when the phone is used. It also provides features including:

- Locate your children
- View Phone Activity & Control Usage
- Block Calls & Spam
- Control Content Based on Age

Verizon, AT&T, T-Mobile, and Sprint each have various plans that cost about $4.99 per month. Remember, they are not the solution to the problem – they are simply part of the solution.

6) **Access Other Parental Controls & Your Wireless Router.**

If your carrier's parental controls don't work for you – you might consider finding "the geek within" and search for other available parental options. There are many on the market that monitor your child's activity, including my favorite, uKnowKids. Although this service won't manage your router – it will arm you with a robust dashboard that familiarizes you with your child's circle of online friends and warns you of any risky or inappropriate online interactions. The cost is less than $10 per month and is all web-based. As such, there is no software that you need to download to your phone, PC or tablet.

Photos and videos that are uploaded to most social media apps such as Instagram, Facebook, Youtube and others will be viewable by you. However, it will not show you what your child is doing on Snap Chat, Kik, and Whatsapp. You can learn more about the apps supported by uknowkids on their customer support page.

ParentKit for IOS is another option for those parents with children using an iPhone or iPad. The program is available for download at the iTunes store.

Regardless of the options – understand that teens are quite creative at navigating their ways around and through parental controls.

If you are somewhat technically savvy, one of the best methods of managing parental controls can often be by configuring them on your router. The router is usually that black, plastic case with all the lights flashing that your broadband or cable company installed at your home. Your router kind of acts like the traffic cop for all the data that passes through your wireless network.

With a little education, understanding your router allows you to provide web filtering for all the devices on your network, including computers, tablets, smartphones and even game consoles with built-in browsers.

Although many routers ship with built-in parental control — not all of them provide such features. If you're one of the lucky ones — the instruction manual might be found in the box or online. Ultimately, the router's configuration will be all done online using a simple browser.

If your router doesn't have such functionality, you can use a FREE service such as OpenDNS to set up parental controls on any router. This might take a little guidance and effort, but to do so, you'll need to change your router's DNS server settings to use OpenDNS. OpenDNS allows you to set up an account and configure web filtering .

Once you're in, you can select various categories of websites to block. Websites you block will redirect to a "This site is blocked" message when visited on your network.

There are many articles related to OpenDNS and other such safeguards. Many point to the fact that OpenDNS is great for blocking websites but not so good for blocking apps on phones and tablets. However, I recommend doing your own research to find the right solution for your family.

A BETTER CHOICE

For most, wrestling with things such as OpenDNS might be too much of a chore. If so, there are other great options such as LUMA, TORCH, and CIRCLE With Disney. My favorite is Circle.

Circle works with your router to aid with the monitoring of your child's internet usage – while also managing their screen time. How cool is that?

Typically, I would associate anything with the name Disney as expensive, quality entertainment, and long lines in the sweltering sun – but disastrously weak in terms of in-home technology. However, in this case, nothing could be further from the truth.

First, the product looks as if it were designed by Apple. It's sleek, simple and elegant in appearance. However, it is in no way shaped like a circle. Rather, it's square with rounded corners. That's where the confusion ends.

Unlike products such as OpenDNS, you don't need a degree in Information Technology or Computer Science to setup and operate.

I often say you wouldn't let your 13-year-old child go to

Times Square by themselves. Yet, Times Square is a great place to take them if they're with a trusted adult. That's essentially the role that Circle with Disney plays. Much like Times Square, the Internet can be a great place for your kids if you are the curator. Circle with Disney helps to enable your role as that TRUSTED ADULT.

The product provides a window into all connected devices that exist on your network. You, in turn, decide what is applicable to each child and their device in terms of screen time and internet choices.

In that respect, it's flexible based on the age or maturity level of each child in your home. You should really take a look at Circle with Disney, and its other service, Circle Go.

7) Automatically Backup Your Child's Photos To The Cloud

One of the great features of my iPhone is how it automatically stores my photos and other information to "the cloud." You can use this feature – and similar features with Android devices – to automatically upload photos, contacts and other information that your child has on their device.

However, if they delete the picture or a contact before it is automatically uploaded, you won't find it in the cloud or your other cloud service. Additionally, if they used Snap Chat to take the picture, it won't be sent to the cloud either unless they stored or copied the picture to their gallery. Regardless, you should consider this as part of the broader strategy of protecting your child's online behavior.

Setting up iCloud for Apple devices is rather easy. You

can learn more by <u>accessing</u> the Apple website.

Verizon and other carriers also offer such services. You can read more about Verizon services which work with many different types of devices by accessing their website and customer support.

8) **Understand & Audit Your Family's Private Information**

We live in a data-driven society. From the time we're born there is data gathered and stored about us. As we grow older and acquire a social security number; enter school; surf the web; register for social media accounts; acquire credit; purchase a home, and take many other actions – data is gathered and stored about each one of us. But where does it go? In reality, it is bought and sold.

From 2010 through 2012, the Wall Street Journal dedicated significant effort to help its readers better <u>understand how data is captured</u>, stored and shared among data analytics and marketing companies.

On April 7th, 2012 WSJ reporters **JULIA ANGWIN** and **JEREMY SINGER-VINE** penned the article titled, <u>SELLING YOU ON FACEBOOK.</u> They beautifully illustrated how mobile apps have changed the landscape of advertising and privacy.

Below is an excerpt that describes the game changer in communication has been the advent of the app.

"Now there are "apps"—stylish, discrete chunks of software that live online or in your smartphone. To "buy" an app, all you have to do is click a button. Sometimes they cost a few dollars, but many apps are free, at least in monetary terms. You often pay in another way. Apps are

gateways, and when you buy an app, there is a strong chance that you are supplying its developers with one of the most coveted commodities in today's economy: personal data."

To assist in both seeing and deleting much of this information about you and your child consider visiting Abine.com.

9) Keep On Top Of Trends

If you're like me, you don't have time to check the weather much less keep track of the latest technology and teen trends. Unfortunately, you need to not only get-up-to-speed – but stay there. Never has technology grown, morphed and taken over large chunks of our lives. As such, it's incumbent on each of us to understand not only the world today – but tomorrow as well.

There are two great resources that will feed you information on a daily basis relative to emerging technological trends... and they're no further than your own device.

Google News allows you to create any number of areas of interest. Simply input the request for articles related to your interest, and you'll receive daily updates. For example, you might be interested in such things as "online privacy," "sexting," "cyberbullying" or "apps."

Flipboard is a tremendous app featuring articles from around the globe on a seemingly infinite amount of topics. Much like Google News, you indicate your area of interest and Flipboard will build your own digital magazine focused on your needs. If you want to better understand the digital life of your teen son or daughter, consider adding Flipboard to your device.

Other news services worth considering include Yahoo News Digest and Circa.

10) Talk To Your Child Again and Again

I can't emphasize enough the importance of having a continued dialog with your child concerning their online activity — and how it can help or hurt them in the future.

I have often used an example from my own life. Up until the time I was 14, we were a middle-class family of six. I had great parents and a brother and two sisters that in many ways were living the American dream. However, life often throws obstacles which are unavoidable. In my case, my father passed away, leaving my mother the heavy task of raising four children without any form of income.

If life were a 100-yard dash, I felt I had to run 120 yards while everyone else in the race was running 100 yards. Life sometimes is not fair.

Your child needs to understand that there will be obstacles in life — but they can avoid self-created obstacles due to their misuse of technology. Mistakes made today might not impact your child next week, next month or next year. So often inappropriate posts, photos, and videos don't surface until the most inopportune time, i.e. When applying for college, that first job interview, when running for public office.

By calmly speaking with them — while trying to understand their circle of friends and use of technology, you stand a much better chance of helping them manage their online personality.

Chapter 8: Conclusion

By now you're exhausted, thinking "Why did we buy that stupid device for our kids? Who knew it could be so difficult?" From my perspective, technology is a great thing for our society – and tremendous for your child. However, it does require management. It does require tough decisions – that impacts the entire family.

You might have one child that you would trust to always do the right thing at age 14. Yet you might have a 17-year-old child you wouldn't trust to send an email. That's why understanding the technology – and how it can best be managed is so important.

Sitting on the floor with our kids in 1985 playing the electronic version of Simon Says still plays out vividly in my mind. The brightly colored flashing lights and rhythmic noise seemed like a page from a Ray Bradbury novel at the time. I never dreamed that the small, plastic, yet seemingly complicated and interactive device would be the precursor of what would evolve into a world of 7×24, online communication, gaming, and entertainment devices that would have almost infinite possibilities.

After nearly 35 years, I realize that Pong and Simon Says were the beginning. Snap Chat, Instagram, and Kik, Musical.ly, Live.ly and WhatsApp is not the end.

For Joseph Wilbrand in 1863, his discovery of trinitrotoluene was the beginning -- not the end. The discovery provided great benefits to society – as well and dreadful consequences. It was the weapon of choice during two world wars. Managed properly, TNT is a valuable power that had made railroads and expressways possible. Managed irresponsibly, it has been responsible for thousands of death and carnage.

Smartphone technology is much the same. Much good has come from its genius. Managed responsibly by families – education and communication soar. Managed irresponsibly -- lives are ruined.

In my 1969 high school Biology class my teacher once said, "The four needs of humans are air, water, food, and shelter." As parents, we must manage access to all of these for our children. In 2017, I might add a 5th need:

"Managing your child's Digital Tattoo."

Research References

Foreword

Wall Street Journal
https://www.wsj.com/articles/SB100014241278873237163045
78480883218514720

A Wired family

www.awiredfamily.org

CNET: A Brief History of Android Phones
https://www.cnet.com/news/a-brief-history-of-android-
phones/

eMarketer: Teen's Ownership of Smartphones Has Surged
https://www.emarketer.com/Article/Teens-Ownership-of-
Smartphones-Has-Surged/1014161

Parents Against Underage Smartphones
http://www.pausamerica.com/

Chapter 1 – A Distracted Society

THE ANDY GRIFFITH SHOW
http://www.imdb.com/title/tt0053479/

Highlights Magazine: State of the Kid
https://www.highlights.com/state-of-the-kid

Stephen King: Children of the Corn
https://en.wikipedia.org/wiki/Children_of_the_Corn

Chapter 2 – The Consequences of Sending Inappropriate Content

Statistic Brain: Sexting & Teens
http://www.statisticbrain.com/sexting-statistics/

Washington Post: Is Sexting The New First Base?
https://www.washingtonpost.com/news/parenting/wp/2014/10/06/sexting-is-the-new-first-base-yes-maybe-even-your-child/?utm_term=.60b98758eaf3

US Library of Medicine: Teens Sexting and its Association with Sexual Behavior
https://www.ncbi.nlm.nih.gov/pmc/articles/PMC3626288/

The New Yorker: The Story of Amanda Todd
http://www.newyorker.com/culture/culture-desk/the-story-of-amanda-todd

Gloria Allred: Dangers of Teen Sexting
http://criminal.lawyers.com/juvenile-law/gloria-allred-dangers-of-teen-sexting.html

Definition: Sextortion
https://en.wikipedia.org/wiki/Sextortion

Trend Micro: Sextortion in The Far east
https://www.trendmicro.de/cloud-content/us/pdfs/security-intelligence/white-papers/wp-sextortion-in-the-far-east.pdf

New York daily News: California Teen Sextortion Plot
http://www.nydailynews.com/news/crime/mastermind-teen-usa-sextortion-plot-18-months-prison-article-1.1724809

The United States Department of Justice: Man Who Extorted Minors Produced Child Pornography Is Sentenced
https://www.justice.gov/usao-ndga/pr/man-who-extorted-minors-produce-child-pornography-sentenced

CBC NEWS: Aydin Coban Sentenced In Netherlands For Fraud & Blackmail
http://www.cbc.ca/news/canada/british-columbia/aydin-coban-sentenced-netherlands-online-fraud-blackmail-1.4027359

IMDB: Shut Up and Dance
http://www.imdb.com/title/tt5709230/

CNN MONEY: Sextortion, Thorn Study
http://money.cnn.com/2016/06/23/technology/sextortion-thorn-study/

WEBPRO NEWS: Microsoft, Teen Sextortion Is Common Online
https://www.webpronews.com/microsoft-teen-sextortion-common-online-2016-09/

Chapter 3 – How and Why Our Private Information Is Invaded

Quara: What Is the Meaning Behind The Quote Plastics in The Graduate?
https://www.quora.com/What-is-the-meaning-behind-the-quote-plastics-from-The-Graduate

Extractmetadata: Metadata Reader
http://www.extractmetadata.com/

PetaPixel: Lawyer Digs Into Instagram's Terms of use
https://petapixel.com/2016/12/07/lawyer-digs-instagrams-terms-use/

Salon: My Embarrassing Picture Went Viral
http://www.salon.com/2013/10/02/my_embarrassing_picture_went_viral/

Introduction of The i-Phone
https://en.wikipedia.org/wiki/IPhone_(1st_generation)

Ashley Madison
https://www.ashleymadison.com/

Have I Been Pawned?
https://haveibeenpwned.com/About

Who Is Ricky Ricardo?
https://en.wikipedia.org/wiki/Desi_Arnaz

Fox News: The Case of Darek Kitlinski
http://www.foxnews.com/politics/2015/07/20/key-lawmaker-demands-answers-from-dea-following-fox-news-report.html

The Letter: Song by Joe Cocker
https://en.wikipedia.org/wiki/The_Letter

What Are Cookies?
https://en.wikipedia.org/wiki/HTTP_cookie

David Patraeus Scandal
https://en.wikipedia.org/wiki/David_Petraeus

New York Times: Hillary Clinton eMail Scandal
https://www.nytimes.com/interactive/2016/05/27/us/politics/what-we-know-about-hillary-clintons-private-email-server.html

SnapChat's Privacy Agreement
https://www.snap.com/en-US/privacy/privacy-policy/

The History of SmarterChild
https://en.wikipedia.org/wiki/SmarterChild

eMarketer: Messaging Apps Reach 1.4 Billion users
https://www.emarketer.com/Article/Mobile-Messaging-Reach-14-Billion-Worldwide-2015/1013215

Venture Beat: Facebook has 11,000 ChatBots
https://venturebeat.com/2016/06/30/facebook-messenger-now-has-11000-chatbots-for-you-to-try/

Fight The New Drug: Internet Porn
http://learn.ftnd.org/

Forbes: Kik Porn Bot Spammers
https://www.forbes.com/forbes/welcome/?toURL=https://www.forbes.com/sites/parmyolson/2014/08/20/kik-porn-bot-spammers/&refURL=&referrer=#6e85c7046f05

TechJunkie: The Best Kik Bots
https://www.techjunkie.com/best-kik-bots/

Using Spoofed Wi-Fi For Mobile Attacks
https://blog.lookout.com/spoofed-wifi-60-minutes

Internet Watch Foundation: Where Do Your Inappropriate Images Go?
https://www.iwf.org.uk/

CNBC: Your SmartPhone Could Be Hacked
https://www.cnbc.com/2016/06/17/your-smartphone-could-be-hacked-without-your-knowledge.html

Gold Frog: Yen VPN Myths Debunked
https://www.goldenfrog.com/blog/myths-about-vpn-logging-and-anonymity

TrickSeek: Free Proxy Servers For School Access
https://www.trickseek.org/free-proxy-sites-list-top-proxy-servers-for-school/

A Wired Family: Parental Controls
https://awiredfamily.org/2016/04/25/managing-your-homes-router-network-beam-me-up-grandma/

Facial Recognition Software
https://en.wikipedia.org/wiki/Facial_recognition_system

The Daily Caller: Facial Recognition Technology Hels NY law Enforcement
http://dailycaller.com/2016/08/29/facial-recognition-technology-helps-ny-law-enforcement-catch-100-identity-thieves/

Tech Target: What Is Machine Learning?
http://whatis.techtarget.com/definition/machine-learning

TechCrunch: Someone Scraped 40,000 Tinder Photographs
https://techcrunch.com/2017/04/28/someone-scraped-40000-tinder-selfies-to-make-a-facial-dataset-for-ai-experiments/

Voactiv: hacked Tinder Photos
http://www.vocativ.com/425644/hacked-tinder-photos-artificial-intelligence-data-research/

What is Google Vision
https://cloud.google.com/vision/

What is Amazon Rekognition?
https://aws.amazon.com/rekognition/?sc_channel=PS&sc_campaign=acquisition_US&sc_publisher=google&sc_medium=rekognition_nb&sc_content=recognition_exact&sc_detail=facial%20recognition%20software&sc_category=rekognition&sc_segment=179121306436&sc_matchtype=e&sc_country=us&s_kwcid=AL!4422!3!179121306436!e!!g!!facial%20recognition%20software&ef_id=WQiPTgAAAo1b4_L8:20170503121457:s

Michele Borba, Ed.D BOOK, Unselfie: Why Empathetic Kids Succeed In An All About Me World
https://www.amazon.com/UnSelfie-Empathetic-Succeed-All-About-Me-World/dp/1501110039/ref=sr_1_1?s=books&ie=UTF8&qid=1452106587&sr=1-1&keywords=unselfie

Indy Star: College Athletes, Your Reputation is Always On the Line
http://www.indystar.com/story/sports/college/indiana/2015/02/26/college-athletes-continue-face-social-media-perils/24054307/

ESPN: The Social Science of Recruiting
http://www.espn.com/college-football/recruiting/story/_/id/14646545/social-media-becomes-powerful-aide-dangerous-connection-recruiting

Chapter 4 - Self Esteem, Stalking, Cat fishing & Divorce

The Guardian: Young Women On Instagram & Self-Esteem
https://www.theguardian.com/media/2015/nov/04/instagram-young-women-self-esteem-essena-oneill

USA TODAY: Sextortion & Teens
https://www.usatoday.com/story/news/nation/2014/07/01/sextortion-teens-online/11580633/

Rise & Stand: What's Illegal & What Isn't In Cyberbullying
http://www.riseandstand.net/whats-illegal-and-whats-not-when-it-comes-to-cyber-harassment/

Computer Fraud & Abuse Act
https://ilt.eff.org/index.php/Computer_Fraud_and_Abuse_Act_(CFAA)

Wired: Teens Sues Over Cyberbullying
https://www.wired.com/2012/04/teen-sues-over-bullying/

Wired: The Story of Lori Drew
https://www.wired.com/2008/11/defendants-daug/

The Atlantic: What the Law Can't Do About Online Harassment
https://www.theatlantic.com/technology/archive/2014/11/what-the-law-can-and-cant-do-about-online-harassment/382638/

Cyberbully Hotline: What is Catfishing?
http://www.cyberbullyhotline.com/catfishing.html

USA TODAY: Manti Teo's Catfish Story Is a Common One
https://www.usatoday.com/story/sports/ncaaf/2013/01/17/manti-teos-catfish-story-common/1566438/

Harpers: Mark Twain
https://harpers.org/author/marktwain/

US Magazine: Curt Schilling Hunts Down Guys Harassing His Daughter
http://www.usmagazine.com/celebrity-news/news/curt-schilling-tracks-down-guys-who-harassed-daughter-on-twitter-201533#ixzz3TL8rqWbp

Reddit/People Magazine: Twenty People Who Lost Their Jobs Due To Social Media
http://people.com/celebrity/employees-who-were-fired-because-of-social-media-posts/

Huffington Post: Divorce & Social Media
http://www.huffingtonpost.com/2015/04/30/way-to-ruin-marriages-facebook_n_7183296.html

Stay Safe Online
https://staysafeonline.org/

Chapter 5 – Pornography

Leave It To Beaver
https://en.wikipedia.org/wiki/Leave_It_to_Beaver

Jacobellis v Ohio
https://en.wikipedia.org/wiki/Jacobellis_v._Ohio

Johannes Gutenberg
https://www.biography.com/people/johannes-gutenberg-9323828

French Post Cards
http://www.wondersandmarvels.com/2016/06/the-naked-truth-about-french-postcards.html

Hugh Heffner & Porn
https://www.biography.com/people/hugh-hefner-9333521

Therapy Associates: Teens & Porn
http://therapyassociates.net/

Newsweek: Japan & Virtual Reality Porn
http://www.newsweek.com/vr-porn-samsung-gear-virtual-reality-477369

Navigating Pornographic Addiction
https://awiredfamily.files.wordpress.com/2017/03/3444d-navigatingpornographyaddiction-aguideforparents.pdf

Nine Things You Should Know About Pornography & the Brain
https://www.bellevue.org/9things-pornography

Chapter 6 – Mental Health

Translational Psychiatry: Sex Differences in Depression
http://www.nature.com/tp/journal/v7/n5/full/tp201710 5a.html?foxtrotcallback=true

Child-Mind Institute
https://childmind.org/

Time Magazine: Why The Kids Are Not Alright
http://time.com/magazine/us/4547305/november-7th-2016-vol-188-no-19-u-s/

Live Science: Will Tech Bring Humanity Together Or Tear it Apart?
https://www.livescience.com/51392-will-tech-bring-humanity-together-or-tear-it-apart.html

The Human Memory
http://www.human-memory.net/brain_neurons.html

Depression & Suicide
https://theworldunplugged.wordpress.com/

Suicide Rates In Palo-Alto
http://www.mercurynews.com/2017/03/03/cdc-report-youth-suicide-rates-in-county-highest-in-palo-alto-morgan-hill/

Philly.com: Does Live Streaming Suicides Influence Our Kids?
http://www.philly.com/philly/health/kids-families/Livestream-suicides-Does-it-influence-our-kids.html

CDC: Suicide Contagion
https://www.cdc.gov/mmwr/preview/mmwrhtml/00031539.htm

TV Series: Thirteen Reasons Why
https://en.wikipedia.org/wiki/13_Reasons_Why

Baltimore Sun: Teens Turns To Social Media For Attention – Even Death

http://www.baltimoresun.com/news/opinion/oped/bs-ed-op-0619-social-media-suicide-20170615-story.html

Twisted Bard: Cyberbullyings Newest Frontier
http://www.twistedbard.com/cyberbullyings-newest-frontier/

Cyberbullying Research Center
https://cyberbullying.org/research.php

Chapter 7 – Managing Your Child's Online Activity

McAfee: Cyberbullying Triple
https://www.mcafee.com/us/about/news/2014/q2/20140603-01.aspx

Huffington Post: Divorce & Social Media
http://www.huffingtonpost.com/2013/06/06/facebook-divorce-linked-i n 3399727.html

Recover
https://recover.org/

Mashable: Seven Apps to Hide Your Sexy Photos
http://mashable.com/2014/09/29/sexting-photo-apps/#Nj5my..e1Pqi

uKnowKids
https://support.uknowkids.com/hc/en-us

ParentKit For OIS
https://parentkit.co/

OpenDNS
www.Opendns.com

Circle with Disney & Circle Go
https://meetcircle.com/

Luma
https://lumahome.com/

Torch
www.mytorch.com

Wall Street Journal: What They Know
http://www.wsj.com/public/page/what-they-know-digital-privacy.html

Raconteur: Where Did My Data Go?
https://www.raconteur.net/technology/where-does-my-data-go

The Guardian: Speak with Your Child About Online Safety
https://www.theguardian.com/technology/2014/aug/11/how-to-keep-kids-safe-online-children-advice

Elite Daily: Why You Should Never take Another Naked Picture
http://elitedaily.com/women/taking-a-selfie-pic-nudie/737323/

The Telegraph: Sexting Myths Busted
http://www.telegraph.co.uk/women/womens-health/10985660/Sexting-scare-6-sexting-myths-busted.html

Chapter 8: Conclusion

Ray Bradbury

https://www.biography.com/people/ray-bradbury-9223240

The Invention of TNT

http://sciencing.com/invention-tnt-15791.html

ABOUT THE AUTHOR

Thanks for taking the time to read our book, SOCIAL MEDIA: YOUR CHILD'S DIGITAL TATTO . I'd like to tell you a little about myself.

First and foremost, I am a father of two wonderful married daughters, a husband to my incredible wife Mary Beth and a grandfather to five beautiful grandchildren. But I'm also a son, brother, uncle, father-in-law, son-in-law, employee, former coach and teacher. As you can see, family and education are my top priorities in life.

However, it is through my experiences in life and education that have allowed me the opportunity to understand the value that technology brings to our lives — as well as the challenges of managing these tools within a framework of families and schools.

My experiences over the past 30 years have been exciting. I started my career as a high school teacher and coach. I later worked at NCR Corporation in Dayton, Ohio for six years as writer and director of video-based and interactive programs related to the computer industry. I worked in the video and film production business for about 20 years before joining the IT Consulting industry in 1999.

I have a Bachelor of Fine Arts Degree from the University of Cincinnati's Design, Art, Architecture & Planning program; a Master's Degree in Education & Communication from Xavier University; Executive Certification in Leadership & Management from The University of Notre Dame and a Masters Certificate in Internet Marketing from the University of San Francisco. I am currently President of A Wired Family.

These experiences and my love of family have been the driving force behind the development of this book and our school speakers program. I hope that you find it of help in managing your child's digital tattoo

Made in the USA
Columbia, SC
31 January 2019